MICHIGAN BUSINESS PAPERS
Number 59

The Department of Economics of Western Michigan University is pleased to cooperate with the Division of Research at the Graduate School of Business Administration, the University of Michigan, in presenting this collection of papers, in which five distinguished economists discuss economic theory and policy as they relate to providing public education. This volume is the eighth in a series being published under these auspices.

MICHIGAN BUSINESS
PAPERS   Number 59

The Economics of Education

Five lectures on economic aspects of public education, given at Western Michigan University under the sponsorship of the Department of Economics, Winter 1973

MYRON H. ROSS, Editor

A publication of the
Division of Research
Graduate School of Business Administration
University of Michigan
Ann Arbor, Michigan

ISBN 087712-106-0

Copyright © 1974
by
The University of Michigan

All rights reserved
Printed in the United States of America

CONTENTS

Preface
  Myron H. Ross ... vii

About the Speakers ... xiii

The Evaluation of Manpower Programs
  Charles C. Killingsworth ... 1

The Integration of Higher Education into the Wage-Labor System
  Samuel Bowles ... 17

How Much and What Kinds of Education for Economic Development?
  Richard Eckaus ... 43

Investments in Ourselves: Opportunities and Implications
  Theodore W. Schultz ... 63

Methods of Finance and the Organization and Administration of Local Schools
  Jerry Miner ... 71

Previous Volumes in This Series ... 91

PREFACE

The relations between education and economics has been a fascinating and important, albeit an underdeveloped, field of study. The pioneering work of T. W. Schultz and Gary Becker among others has reduced the extent of underdevelopment, but much remains to be done. Despite the importance of education, many significant questions of theory and policy remain unresolved.

This volume of papers is based upon the lecture series given at Western Michigan University in the winter of 1973 by eminent economists. It continues a relationship between Western Michigan University and the School of Business Administration of the University of Michigan, being the eighth such volume to be published by the Division of Research at the University of Michigan Graduate School of Business Administration. Previous volumes in the series and their contents are listed in the Appendix.

Some unifying threads run through the present five lectures. First, it is recognized that there is a difficult "identification" problem. No one doubts that education and economic growth are related. But does education produce growth, or does growth produce education? Secondly, all the authors are antiromantic, or, perhaps more correctly, nonromantic, in their approach to education. None views education as the *deus ex machina* bringing us to the gates of heaven; rather, all share the assumption that the structuring of an effective educational system must be based upon careful reasoning and valid empirical data. Third, in the tradition of economics, they draw a clear-cut distinction between questions of efficiency and equity. Economists feel at home with questions of efficiency, but they have difficulty with questions of equity—as, alas, who doesn't?

Charles C. Killingsworth relates manpower policy to general economic policy. He sees manpower programs as necessary, though not sufficient, elements in a successful economic policy. Professor Killingsworth points to the element of fashion in public opinion of manpower programs. Ten years ago these programs were considered the "cure," and currently they are viewed with great suspicion.

His call is for a more balanced view of manpower programs than we have experienced over the past decade. He cites the fact that in any benefit-cost analysis it is quite easy to engage in the fallacy of emphasis, for instance to focus almost solely on benefits with little attention paid to costs or vice versa. He also calls for an end to the double standard which requires that manpower programs justify their existence by empirical documentation but takes no such approach with regard to monetary and fiscal policy. As testament to Killingsworth's view, the hung (and confused) jury regarding the question of the effectiveness of the 1968 tax increase is a case in point.

Professor Killingsworth also points out how manpower programs "solve" the unemployment problem by statistical legerdemain. That is, if current manpower programs were eliminated, the unemployment rate would rise about 0.8 percent, because enrollees in manpower programs are considered employed rather than unemployed.

R. S. Eckaus addresses himself to the problem of planning manpower for less-advanced economies. Two general themes are found in his discussion. First, he underscores that education, like "free lunches," is not free. It takes scarce resources. But, given the overdeveloped political propensity to curry favor with the public, it is nevertheless quite easy, from an economic point of view, to waste resources on education. Secondly, Professor Eckaus emphasises some of the limitations inherent in educational and manpower planning. Many of these points recall to mind von Hayek's critique of socialist planning many decades ago. Educational planning is complex and in many cases requires more information than is available.

The less-advanced economy, Eckaus points out, has a menu of three broad approaches for planning for manpower requirements. First, it may "follow the leader." After all, there are established and on-going educational systems in the more-developed economies—so why not emulate these systems? This approach requires an answer to the question of which leader to follow. The British? The French? Following some advanced nation's pattern of education also contains a great risk of producing an excess of college graduates—witness the oversupply of lawyers and economists in much of the less-developed world. And a pool of unemployed economists and lawyers may be politically disruptive.

A second approach is the manpower approach. This involves a simple linear "production function" approach. The problem is to project future national outputs and extrapolate future labor requirements. There are, however, difficulties. Eckaus points out that there is no simple production function which can be applied at all times and in all places. For instance, whether midwives or M.D.'s perform the obstetric function will depend not only on factor prices and the level of income but on cultural differences, which will impose different requirements.

Finally, there is the rate-of-return approach. With this approach the advice is to expand that type of training which has an above average rate of return and decrease that type of training which has a below average rate of return. Eckaus points out that, while this approach is impeccable from a logical point of view, it fails because adequate information on benefits and costs is not available.

Samuel Bowles's lecture, in contrast to the other lectures in the series, discusses the relation of education to the economy as well as to society, in a systematic way and with an extended historical discussion of educational developments. He emphasizes that with the development of higher education greater and greater contradictions have developed in the capitalist system. Bowles sees the educational system as a tool of the capitalist class. The educational system not only serves the capitalist class by providing trained and obedient workers, but it also serves to ameliorate class conflict. Thus, he contends, students steered into community colleges through the use of testing and counseling procedures, are programmed for failure.

He predicts that two trends which tend to radicalize students will be strengthened in the next decade. The first is the increase in enrollments from secondary to higher education, which has escalated serious class inequality by increasing the number of nonelite college students. Bowles expects more and more conflict between the elite and the nonelite students, with the latter attempting to gain equality with the former. The second trend is the reduced importance of income differences between the professional and white-collar worker, on one hand, in contrast with the blue-collar worker, on the other. More and more, he contends, the working conditions of the professional have begun to resemble that of a production line.

Bowles's theme that education is contradictory and that its growth produces pressure for social change follows a long tradition—witness the writing of Marx, Veblen, and Schumpeter.

Jerry Miner discusses financing of local schools. His approach is broader than that taken by the commonly heard discussions of school finance, because he integrates reform of financial structure of schools with changing the structure and governance of local schools. In discussing school finance in the United States, he emphasizes that equalization of expenditure or tax effort will not necessarily produce equality. Since school expenditures are roughly 45 percent of local government expenditures, however, any reform of school finance will ease local government financial problems.

The United States is unique in having no national educational standards, Miner points out. The common pattern in Europe is that national standards for K-12 precede considerations of finance. This practice ameliorates inequities resulting from differences in wealth.

Certain other differences between U.S. and European educational policies are also evident, and we cannot rule out the possibility that the European policies may be superior. Miner points out that there is greater equality of education provided in Europe than in the United States. Further, the European systems generally have accommodated or incorporated the originally independent denominational schools. There is no "parochiaid" issue in most Western European countries.

The pattern of private schools in the Netherlands, with many elements of the voucher system, is particularly interesting. What is surprising is that the system has not produced great diversity in educational patterns. Perhaps this is related to the fact that the population of the Netherlands is highly homogenous to begin with.

T. W. Schultz discusses a subject he has long been associated with in the literature, namely, the educational investment process. He divides the issue into the question of efficiency and the question of equity.

With regard to the question of efficiency, he points out that students are very efficient in allocating their resources; in fact, he goes so far as to say that "college students are in general as efficient in this context as firms for profit are in their domain." Consistent with recent evidence on rates of return in education, Schultz stresses that more funds should be invested in lower levels of schooling compared to those that go into higher education.

Schultz makes the interesting point that university research is a public good and if we want it in sufficient quantity this activity must be financed by society. In sharp contrast to Bowles's position, Schultz holds that the prime issue in education is one of efficiency, and that the educational system is probably a poor vehicle for redistributing the nation's income, if that is desired.

Schultz dicusses the present difficulties experienced by colleges and universities because the boom in enrollments has passed. During the boom there was overinvestment in physical plants and expensive equipment. In addition, the past boom has produced present difficulties because promotions were easy, and colleges are now stuck with many high-ranking tenured faculty.

Schultz argues the benefits of higher education are overstated and, to the extent that they exist, they are primarily received by the student rather than by society. "Most college students" he states, "should be paying the *full cost* of the instruction they receive." (Emphasis added.)

Acknowledgments

The editor is indebted to the participants in the lecture series for their fine cooperation. Financial support for the lecture series was obtained with the guidance and cooperation of Dean Cornelius Loew and Prof. Robert Bowers, Head of the Department of Economics. Particular thanks should be extended to the Visiting Lecturers Committee during the 1972-73 academic year—Professors Wayland Gardner and Werner Sichel. The timely preparation of the manuscript would not have been possible without the assistance of Mrs. Em Hollingshead and Mrs. Cress Strand. Deep appreciation is expressed for the editorial work of Mrs. Henrietta Slote of the Division of Research at the Graduate School of Business Administration, the University of Michigan.

M. H. R.

Western Michigan University
July 1973

ABOUT THE SPEAKERS

CHARLES C. KILLINGSWORTH *is University Professor of Labor and Industrial Relations at Michigan State University, where he has been a member of the faculty since 1947. He has served as Chairman of the University's Department of Economics and also as Director of its Labor and Industrial Relations Center.*

Before 1947 Dr. Killingsworth was on the faculty at Johns Hopkins University, and he was also Chief of the Analytical Studies Unit of the Social Security Administration. From October 1952 to April 1953 he was on leave of absence from Michigan State University in order to serve as a member and as Chairman of the National Wage Stabilization Board. Earlier, during World War II, he served on a number of dispute panels established by the War Labor Board.

Dr. Killingsworth is a past president of the National Academy of Arbitrators. He has served as an arbitrator in a large number of labor disputes since 1943 and as a permanent arbitrator and an umpire for various corporations and unions. In addition, Dr. Killingsworth has been on advisory committees for governors of Michigan and for the U.S. Department of Labor. He is currently a member of the National Manpower Policy Task Force.

He is the author of State Labor Relations Acts, *published in 1948 by the University of Chicago Press; he is coauthor of* Trade Union Publications, *published in 1944 by Johns Hopkins Press, and of* Structure of American Industry, *published in 1954 by Macmillan (second revised edition, 1961). Dr. Killingsworth received his A. B. degree from Missouri State College, his master's degree from Oklahoma State University, and the Ph.D. degree in Economics from the University of Wisconsin.*

SAMUEL BOWLES *is Associate Professor of Economics at Harvard University, where he is also Research Associate at both the Center for International Affairs and the Center for Educational Policy Research. He holds the B.A. degree from Yale University and the Ph.D. from Harvard.*

Dr. Bowles is a widely published author. He has written extensively on the efficent allocation of educational resources, on the role of education in national development, and on the intergenerational reproduction of economic inequality. His works have been translated into Spanish, French, Hungarian, and Japanese.

Dr. Bowles has also served as an education officer for the government of Northern Nigeria (1960-62); as a development adviser to the government of Greece, 1966; and as a visiting lecturer at the Instituto de Economia, Universidad de la Habana.

RICHARD S. ECKAUS has been Professor of Economics at Massachusetts Institute of Technology since 1962. He was Research Associate at the M.I.T. Center for International Studies from 1952-69. A graduate of Iowa State University, Dr. Eckaus holds the M.A. in Economics from Washington University (St. Louis) and the Ph.D., also in Economics, from M.I.T. His interest in the relation of education to questions of economics and national development is long standing. He has worked on research projects in New Delhi and Rome, and he has also conducted research for the Organization of American States. He has served as a consultant to the Agency for International Development and as a member of the Board of Economic Advisers to the Governor of Massachusetts. Dr. Eckaus has been awarded grants by the Rockefeller Foundation, the Social Science Research Council, and the Ford Foundation; and he has held a Guggenheim Fellowship.

From 1969-71 Dr. Eckaus served the Carnegie Commission for Higher Education in its study of the returns to education. He is the author of numerous articles and has written and edited several books.

THEODORE W. SCHULTZ, whose achievements during his long career as teacher, author, and practicing economist are well known, has been Charles L. Hutchinson Distinguished Service Professor in the Department of Economics at the University of Chicago since 1952. Holding the B.S. degree from Oklahoma State College and the M.S. and Ph.D. degrees from the University of Wisconsin, Dr. Schultz served as Professor of Argricultural Economics and as Head of the Department of Economics and Sociology at Iowa State College before joining the University of Chicago faculty in 1943. He was Chairman of the Department of Economics at Chicago from 1946-61.

Dr. Schultz has served the U.S. government since 1929 as adviser, consultant, and mission leader for a variety of departments and agencies. Most notably, perhaps, he has served the Agency for International Development *as a member of its Advisory Committee on Economic Development, conducting studies of agricultural and technological development in Central Europe, Russia, Scandinavia, Scotland, and Latin America.*

His extensive writings, which include eleven books, deal with the economics of agriculture, national development, and education.

Dr. Schultz is a past president of the American Economic Association and a Founding Member of the National Academy of Education; he has held positions of official responsibility in many of the professional organizations to which he has belonged, among them the National Bureau of Economic Research, the Committee for Economic Development, and the Institute for Current World Affairs. He is currently a Trustee of the Population Council and of the National Planning Association.

JERRY MINER *is Professor of Economics at the Maxwell School of Citizenship and Public Affairs, Syracuse University. He received the B.A., M.A., and Ph.D. degrees at the University of Michigan. He has served as Senior Research Economist in the Social Research Department of UNESCO and as Visiting Research Fellow in the Higher Education Research Unit of the London School of Economics and Political Science.*

Dr. Miner has written a wide range of books and other publications which deal with the economics of education, including articles which appeared in the Encyclopedia of Education, *Vol. III, and* The World Yearbook of Education, 1967. *At present he is a consultant to the National Academy of Sciences, Committee on Training Grants to Bioscientists, and he is Director of both the Maxwell Program in the Economics of Education and the Joint Maxwell-Upstate Medical Center Program in Health Services.*

THE EVALUATION OF MANPOWER PROGRAMS

CHARLES C. KILLINGSWORTH

As I listened to the chairman's introduction, it occurred to me that one biographical detail should be added for this occasion. Ten years ago this month I became chairman of the Michigan Manpower Development Committee, which had the function of advising the governor on the administration of manpower programs in Michigan. Mainly because of the strong support of the governor, Michigan was among the national leaders in getting manpower programs launched ten years ago under the Manpower Development and Training Act, then newly passed.

The relevance of this bit of history is that ten years ago there was vast enthusiasm about the prospects for manpower training, not only in Michigan but clear across the nation. There was some argument among economists as to which approach was going to do the greater job—tax-cutting and other aspects of fiscal policy, or these more direct kinds of program like manpower training. But among the manpower-training advocates by and large there was strong enthusiasm. Indeed, among those advocates in the Congress there was something that approached overenthusiasm. One might almost have thought that they were talking about some kind of patent medicine that was guaranteed to cure almost everything. At one time or another in Congress manpower training was held out as the cure, not only for unemployment, but for poverty and alienation and inflation—and there were perhaps half a dozen other ills that somebody or other in Congress was promising manpower programs would cure or at least very greatly help.

My topic, the evaluation of manpower programs, is one that I suggested several months ago. If this discussion had been scheduled for a few months from now, it might have turned out to be an autopsy. There are strong rumors coming out of Washington now that rather drastic decisions have been made concerning the manpower programs; the reports are that—by and large, with very few exceptions—these programs are going to be drastically cut back and in some cases entirely eliminated. I won't go into all the gossip and reports that have been coming out, but let me say that some of them seem to have a disturbing authenticity. Now, I think there may be some connection between this excessive euphoria of ten years ago that I just mentioned and the situation that we are apparently confronting here in the early months of 1973.

What is badly needed right now is a careful, unemotional look at what manpower programs have accomplished, what they have not accomplished, what we might expect them to accomplish, and what it is unreasonable to expect them to accomplish. Thus we might try to get some appreciation of the proper role of manpower programs in a national employment policy. My conception of employment policy is that among other things it includes fiscal and monetary policy to the extent that this policy is used to promote employment. I want to emphasize my belief that intelligent use of fiscal and monetary policy is an absolutely indispensable part of any employment policy, although it is not sufficient in itself to constitute the entirety of employment policy. I believe that there must be other measures, manpower programs and additional measures, and the really important problem is to discover the proper balance, the proper emphasis between fiscal and monetary policy, manpower programs, and other kinds of program, such as job creation.

Current Administrative Views of Manpower Programs

But, to come back to the more immediate problem, I think we have in Washington today a rather widespread conviction among some highly placed officials and among some program administrators, at both the national and local levels, that manpower programs just have not worked. Why should we have such a feeling? Well, I believe that there are three or four reasons for the development of this view, and I've already mentioned one of them. That is, some people in the Congress and perhaps to some extent people outside the Congress, who seemed to promise much too much from manpower programs, raised expectations unreasonably high. A second reason for the view, I believe, is that some manpower programs have unquestionably failed, and I want to go into those failures (or at least extremely disappointing performances) and consider some of the reasons for them. But some people have generalized from one or two isolated instances to cover the whole program, not an uncommon kind of fallacy.

Review of evaluation studies

There have been allegedly scholarly studies which have constituted harsh attacks on manpower programs. I had the misfortune last summer to agree to review a very thick manuscript produced by one of the so-called public interest law firms in Washington, the theme of which was that the whole manpower program was a fraud and a rip-off. The "study" alleged that the federal government, with the connivance of local officials, has used the manpower program simply to keep the poor in their place and to make people think something was happening when actually absolutely nothing was happening, except possibly the training of a few people for menial, low-paid jobs. This is, of course, a rather extreme example, but I think that even reckless charges of this kind are having some effect.

Finally, there seems to be some tendency in the Administration and in Congress as well to look only at the outlays or costs of the programs and to ignore the benefits. It's a little as if General Motors in preparing its annual report reported all the outlays to employees and to suppliers and so on and failed to include in its report the payments it received from the purchasers of its products. There are monetary benefits to be gained from these manpower programs. You don't always have a situation in which the returns exceed the costs, but it seems to me highly fallacious social cost accounting to look solely at the costs of a program of this kind and to ignore the benefits. So I want to place some emphasis on the cost/benefit ratio, not because I think these calculations tell the whole story, not because I think they are infallible, but simply because they present a side of this story which has been rather neglected in a great deal of the discussion, particularly in the last year or so.

I have been speaking rather broadly of manpower programs. Let me focus on one type of manpower program, the training program. Since 1961 we've had an apparently enormous growth in overall manpower programs, and one can be somewhat misled by most of the summaries of the growth of these programs. The figure usually cited as the total expenditure for manpower programs in 1961 is $250 million—one-quarter billion dollars—and the estimate for fiscal 1973 is placed as $5 billion, which would seem to indicate a twenty-fold expansion. But the picture changes a little when you look at the details of the expenditure for 1973. Roughly a billion dollars of the $5 billion goes for vocational education and vocational rehabilitation. Of course these are worthwhile programs, but they have been in existence for many years, and they are not primarily aimed at the hard-core unemployed, although the programs of the past ten years have included such an emphasis. Another half-billion dollars goes for Employment Service operations, an activity now of nearly forty years' standing. About $400 million goes for child care; a billion and a quarter goes for the Emergency Employment Act, quite a different kind of manpower program, which is, in a sense, a new departure. So, of the $5 billion budget, we have about $3 billion going for activities *other* than manpower training in the conventional sense. We have about $2 billion left for that kind of program. Now, an expansion from $250 million to $2 billion is rather large, but it is obviously not an expansion of $250 million to $5 billion. I want to come back to this point in a few minutes, but just bear in mind if you will that many discussions of the total amount that is being spent for manpower training as such contain considerable exaggeration.

How useful are these manpower-training programs? Because they have been in operation for ten years, generating lots of numbers, and because money has also been available for their evaluation, we have had a large number of evaluation studies. The studies are not all of high quality. Some, to be perfectly frank, are pretty poor, especially a few from the early years. And only a minute fraction of the specific manpower-training programs have been studied. But over the years the evaluators have learned something about technique; they've become much more careful; although they haven't entirely solved certain problems, they've learned from each other and from experience how to meet them.

A basic problem, just to anticipate a little, is to find a good control group. If you have, let's say, 100 people who are going into a manpower-training program this month and you want to measure the effects of the training, you have to try to figure out what would have happened to these people in the absence of the training program. You can't do that by a simple "before-and-after" comparison, using only the particular group that gets the training. You have to have some sort of control group that matches the training group in all important characteristics except that it will not have had the training. Then you compare the post-training experience of the trainees and the experience of those in the control group during the same time period, and you attribute the differences that you discover to the training. The simple before-and-after comparison has the major disadvantage of ignoring contemporaneous changes in the national economy.

Also connected with evaluation studies are some rather difficult technical problems about social discount rates that I won't even try to explain here this evening. There are other problems in estimating benefits of the training. Over how long a period are you going to assume that the benefits of training last? Does a man benefit for ten years or twenty years or thirty years? Well, like true academicians, the evaluators usually give you all three figures and let you take your choice. It's sometimes hard for an academician to make a tough choice of that kind, and so he leaves it to the reader.

The differences between methods of choosing control groups,

differences in choices of discount rates, differences in the length of benefit periods—all of these factors make cross-study comparisons difficult. But I'm going to be a bit unscientific. Having warned you of these shortcomings of the evaluation studies, I'm going to generalize, to give you what seems to me to be a rather solid consensus that has emerged from evaluation studies of the last ten years, particularly so far as the manpower-training programs are concerned. Then I want to turn to some more specialized types of program and particularly a couple of programs that have turned out to be at best disappointing and at the worst clear failures.

The surprising thing that emerges from an across-the-board review of these evaluation studies is that in almost all cases the primary finding is that the cost/benefit ratios are quite favorable. There is a very widespread impression to the contrary, a fairly general belief that the spending for these programs greatly exceeds any possible returns. But if you look at a tabulation of studies, studies of studies, and so on, you find estimated cost benefit ratios that run from 1.5- up to 8-, 10-, 12-, and, in an extreme case, as high as a 15-fold return of benefits as compared with the costs of the program.

I should emphasize again that not all programs have been evaluated. Furthermore, some particular programs in some localities have shown a return of less than one. The Job Corps is an interesting example. Some of the early studies of the Job Corps turned up rather unfavorable cost/benefit ratios. Some later critics of these evaluation studies discovered that all of the capital costs of the program, which were very substantial, were being charged to the first year's trainees. That is an unusual method of accounting, and it made the costs for those first-year trainees extremely high. When you had a more realistic type of accounting for capital costs and spread the capital costs over several years, the cost/benefit ratios, even for the Job Corps, turned out to be not too bad—low compared to the other training programs but still above 1. And, as one of the evaluators pointed out, that seemed to be a fairer and more realistic way of judging the merit of the Job Corps than the favored Congressional method of comparing the cost of a year in the Job Corps with the cost of a year at Harvard.

Let me move from the specific back to the general and again emphasize the basic fact that the consensus is fairly broad among those who have actually analyzed the programs and those who have studied the evaluation studies: the cost/benefit ratios are quite good. As a matter of fact, one of the researchers was moved to wonder why it was that the private capital market had not taken over the financing of these programs. The rate of return, he observed, is so much higher than the rate of return in, say, manufacturing, that it looked as if a real opportunity was being ignored by private entrepreneurs.

There is an important exception to the foregoing consensus. Probably the most influential single evaluation study of a manpower-training program is one that has not been published, although it appears to have had a considerable impact on the thinking of some key policy-makers in Washington. The study, done by a staff member of the U.S. Department of Labor, utilized Social Security records of manpower program trainees to compare their post-training earnings with those of a sample of other workers covered by Social Security who supposedly had characteristics comparable to those of the trainees. The study's key finding was that the training was of little or no benefit to most categories of trainees, at least so far as earnings were concerned. But this study has one basic technical deficiency. When a highly qualified statistician who recently retired from a high government post reviewed the study, he concluded that there was serious doubt that the comparison groups used in the study were really, in all significant characteristics, comparable to the trainees. The reviewer also made some comparisons of his own, using the same data but with what he regarded as more plausible criteria for the selection of comparison groups; and his findings were markedly different—that is, he found evidence of quite substantial gains from training. I have had the opportunity to examine both the original study and the review, and I find the reviewer's criticisms quite persuasive. It is indeed ironic that the one substantial study with negative findings—a study that has not been published and which rests upon a vulnerable methodology—appears to carry more weight in high official circles than all of the other more defensible studies with findings that are strongly favorable to manpower training.

Evaluation of program results and emphases

One of the shortcomings in the recent administration of manpower-training programs has been a rather decided shift in emphasis within the overall total. The shift in emphasis has been in exactly the opposite direction from that which would seem to be suggested by attention to these evaluation studies. Let me give you an example.

OJT under MDTA compared to JOBS. A program which has among the highest rates of return is on-the-job training under the Manpower Development and Training Act. We use the alphabetical jargon, OJT under MDTA. That's really a great program, and there are good reasons why, including high selectivity of trainees. But, be that as it may, strictly on cost-benefit analysis, it scores a very high rating. One of the poorest programs has been the so-called JOBS program (Job Opportunities in the Business Sector), which subsidizes employment with private employers who develop their own selection, training, counseling, and other programs. There are some understandable reasons for its very poor record, but the fact remains that JOBS is not very effective. Quite a lot of money has been shifted out of OJT, the high-return program, and put into the low-return JOBS program. The shift is impossible to understand unless you make the assumption that there is a private-sector bias at work here; and I would suggest that such an assumption may not be unreasonable. I think I have detected that particular bias, not only in the present Administration, but in the last Administration and the Administration before that. In fact a nonconformist like John Kenneth Galbraith would argue that the training of most economists, today as in the past, predisposes them to a private-sector bias.

WIN program. A different kind of manpower-training program—one with a training component but with different organization, a different set of goals, and certainly a different outcome from the conventional manpower-training programs—is the so-called WIN (Work Incentive) program. This quite large and costly program was designed to get AFDC mothers off the welfare rolls by providing a combination of training and financial incentives which many officials predicted would move very large numbers of AFDC recipients into jobs. The program started in 1969, and some of its returns are just now beginning to come in.

I will summarize the results of the first two years of the program's operation. By the fall of 1971, 2.7 million AFDC recipients had been assessed, that is, they had sat down with a government agent who had rather carefully examined their work readiness and their possibilities of securing employment. Of these 2.7 million, about one-quarter (24 percent) were found to be appropriate for referral to the WIN program. But of that group, only about 60 percent were actually referred and enrolled in the WIN program; there was a lot of attrition along the way. So we have dropped from 2.7 million to fewer than 400,000 actually enrolled in the WIN program. Of this group, fewer than 80,000, or about 20 percent of the enrollees, completed the course of training. Of those that completed the training, 50,000 were placed in jobs; but of the 50,000, only 27,000 remained employed after six months, and by no means all of those who got jobs earned enough to move off the welfare rolls.

So if you look at the 2.7 million people that were run through the first stage of this program and then look at the final result, 27,000 of them with reasonably steady jobs, the success rate is only 1 percent. If you consider only the number actually enrolled in the program, then you still get a success rate of only 7 percent. The Department of Labor estimated that the overall costs of the program per placement (the 50,000 trainees placed in jobs, not the 27,000 who held onto jobs for six months or more) came to $5,000. That cost is considerably in excess of the cost, per trainee placed, of the great majority of manpower-training programs.

Now several things should be said about this experience. In the first place, the goals of the WIN program were never very clearly specified. In the second place, the clientele from which enrollees were being drawn—mainly young mothers, a majority of whom were white, but with a large minority of blacks—was not the clientele that is most promising so far as prospects of success in the labor markets are concerned. Many of the women have legitimate household duties. They have to take care of young children and for that reason cannot reasonably be considered appropriate material for the program. But in my judgment the greatest fallacy of the entire program was the assumption that, if we merely provided training and a financial incentive for these mothers, the labor market would see to it that there were jobs available at the end of the training period. Well, this was a ludicrous assumption under which to start a program in the year 1969. The country fell into a recession in the latter part of 1969, with employment falling off and the unemployment rate rising. It is quite possible that this whole program might have worked better in a period of expanding employment opportunities, but we don't really know.

This experience points up some important considerations in the operation of almost any kind of manpower program. The choice of enrollees makes a very real difference. This point may seem to be terribly obvious, but it certainly wasn't obvious ten years ago, and it is not obvious to many of the critics of these programs today. The design of the program also has an effect. If you design a training program that is unrelated to any occupational demand in the labor market, the trainees will have a hard time finding jobs—another obvious point, but apparently we have to learn the hard way. Some of the WIN training suffered from that defect. Still another lesson of the WIN experience is that when the general labor market is going sour, with the unemployment rate rising rapidly, trainees—particularly welfare mothers—don't stand a very good chance of finding jobs. And I might say that other examples from other programs involving nonwelfare people and other time periods support these general, obvious points.

Public Service Employment under the Emergency Employment Act. Let me mention, finally, another recent program—Public Service Employment under the Emergency Employment Act. I believe that some kinds of public service employment program may properly be classified as manpower programs. But the assumptions and the objectives are quite different from those of manpower training. Let me preface my comments on the current Emergency Employment Act by saying that for many years now I have been one of those advocating public service employment as one of the remedies for unemployment. I have testified before committees of Congress, I've lobbied my congressman, and I've talked to various people who might have some influence on decision making. There have been many others who have campaigned for public service employment as a part of a properly developed employment policy in the United States. So I was pleased when Congress finally acted on this kind of program. I now have to say that I am pretty well disappointed today. I'm not disillusioned with the concept of public service employment, but I am disappointed with the way in which the current embodiment has worked out in practice.

The present Emergency Employment Act was passed in 1971 following a Presidential veto of a similar measure in 1970. Without going into detail, let me simply say that the second bill was drafted with an eye to avoiding a possible veto; therefore, many of the President's objections were given very great weight, and the design of the measure was considerably changed from what it had been in the 1970 bill. Further, the drafters of the revised bill wanted to pick up as many votes as possible in the Congress in order to override a veto if necessary. So what we got was a kind of catch-all measure that promised many people many things—much more than could be delivered, given the funding and the nature of the program. This "something-for-everybody" approach is responsible for some of what I see as shortcomings of the emergency program.

However, there are some good things that ought to be said for the program. It was launched with almost record speed; as you all know, the slowness of bureaucracy in starting up a new program is almost legendary. Congress acted on the appropriation bill for this legislation on 6 August 1971, and the day after Labor Day the first people were hired under the new program, which is really dazzling speed compared with some past performances. The Department of Labor and the localities followed through, and it was only a very few months until the maximum employment was achieved. From some standpoints that achievement was highly desirable, because we were still in a recession at the time and the purely fiscal boost from this new payroll was beneficial. And, from all appearances, those hired were assigned useful work.

As the program has worked out, however, there are some serious shortcomings in it. I want to give you just one set of figures to illustrate my most basic criticism, which relates to the kind of people who got jobs under the program. I think that it is quite meaningful to classify workers by educational attainment. People with less than 12 years of education are roughly the bottom third of the labor force, and the people with one or more years of college represent approximately the upper third of the labor force. But the bottom third experienced almost half of the unemployment (44 percent) in 1972, and the top third less than a fifth (19 percent). Of the Emergency Employment Act hires, only 24 percent came from the bottom group, which was accounting for nearly half the unemployment; and 31 percent came from the top group, which was accounting for only a fifth of the unemployment. This is certainly not the outcome that had been sought by the long-time advocates of public service employment. Their greatest emphasis had been on providing opportunities for the hard-core unemployed. What developed under the Emergency Employment Act was a quite disproportionate emphasis on the hiring of people with college training and relatively low unemployment and a real skimping on the hiring of people with below-average education and above-average unemployment rates.

So we have to conclude that the Emergency Employment Act as it now stands is not really a program for the disadvantaged; it is more a kind of revenue-sharing program. I made that comment to the Assistant Secretary of Labor in charge of the program and he readily agreed with it. The only limitation in this program that you don't find in the general revenue-sharing program is that all the money has to be spent on wages. Beyond that, there's very little in the way of effective limitation. Now of course there are many priority groups—veterans, blacks, disadvantaged, and various other preference groups—but there are so many that the preferences become almost meaningless. The most significant priority is the one for veterans, and—whatever its merits—that priority has compelled discrimination against women. About three-quarters of the EEA hires have been men, and one-quarter women.

The point that this program is another form of revenue sharing is of some importance, because there have been some rather explicit suggestions that the new $30 billion general revenue-sharing program will have a large and beneficial effect on the labor market. It may increase employment on balance; but I think that there is no reason to believe that even a proportionate share of the jobs will go to the most disadvantaged members of the labor force. The disadvantaged are likely to get a less than proportionate benefit from expenditures under general revenue sharing—just as has happened under the Emergency Employment Act.

I think we have to recognize that it is perfectly reasonable and logical for mayors and other local administrators to hire the "cream" of the unemployed when they get EEA or other revenue-sharing funds for payrolls. It would be close to a dereliction of duty if they did otherwise, so long as they have a virtually free choice in the matter. My criticisms of the outcome of the EEA experience should not be interpreted as a conclusion that we should abandon this approach to the unemployment problem. The real lesson, in my opinion, is that we should recast the law to insure preference for the most disadvantaged among the unemployed. There are several rather obvious ways to do this. One is for the federal government to take all responsibility for hiring and then to offer the services of those hired to local authorities for properly designed projects. Another approach is to specify the target groups much more clearly and then to monitor the local hiring authorities closely to insure that the jobs go to the right people. The disappointing experience under the Emergency Employment Act has not altered my conviction that job creation for the disadvantaged is an essential component of an adequate employment policy.

I want to make one last comment to put the Emergency Employment Act in perspective. Our last big effort in this field was back in the 1930s with the WPA, the CCC, and NYA, and other programs of that sort. I think most people today are quite uninformed about the relative size of those programs. Even though we had much higher unemployment levels then, we had a very much larger proportion of the unemployed enrolled in the work relief programs. In fact, if you look at the years when these programs were in full force and effect—from about 1934 through 1939—you see that they provided jobs for 35 to 43 percent of the unemployed workers. This year the Emergency Employment Act is providing jobs for 3 percent of the unemployed. You can look at it in relation to the size of the labor force. The work relief programs of the 1930s involved about 7 percent of the total civilian labor force. The 1971-72 program, at its maximum size of 170,000 jobs, involved two-tenths of one percent (0.2 percent) of the civilian labor force.

Weakness of Manpower Programs to Date

That observation brings me to a more general point about the manpower programs. I believe these programs are weak in that they have failed to accomplish what many of us had hoped they would have accomplished by now, but I have not yet touched on what I regard as the principal source of their weakness. Their shortcoming lies not in selection of enrollees, not in the design of the training programs, not even in the state of the labor market; rather it lies in their small scale, compared to the need for these programs.

Scale of programs

About 1966 or 1967 the Department of Labor undertook a study to estimate the potential clientele for manpower programs as of that time. The estimate included not only those officially counted as unemployed but also the hidden unemployed, those who don't get counted in the official surveys but who are willing and able to work. The estimates also included the so-called sub-employed, those who were working a full year at a job without earning enough to rise above the property level, and it included various other groups. The study came up with the rather startling finding that about 13 million people were probably eligible for enrollment in manpower programs. At that time the total number of slots available was between 600,000 and 700,000. In other words, the opportunities provided amounted to about 5 percent of those eligible to enroll. In the ten years from 1963 to 1972, there were about 8 million first-time enrollments in training and work programs, but only about 3.5 million of them were in programs that had a significant training component.[1]

Another way of looking at the scale of our manpower-training efforts is to consider the dollars spent on this activity as compared with some other kinds of expenditure. The total amount spent on all kinds of work and training programs administered by the U.S. Department of Labor from 1963 to 1972 is $9.5 billion, and a little less than $6 billion of that went to programs with a substantial training component. Compare that, if you will, with the cumulative value of the great tax cut of 1964, which was sold mainly as a remedy for excessive unemployment. A fairly conservative estimate would be that the federal government has foregone about $150 billion in tax revenues as a result of that one tax cut (and there were some other cuts later). I have never seen any proof that cutting taxes is 25 times as effective as manpower training in reducing unemployment. Yet that seems to be the implicit assumption which underlies this enormous disparity of emphasis between manpower training and tax cutting.

We seem to have developed a rather blatant double standard in employment policy. Many advocates of fiscal policy as the sovereign remedy for unemployment apparently believe that nothing more than bald assertion is necessary to establish the effectiveness of tax cutting, and some of the same people demand proof beyond a shadow of doubt that manpower training is effective. Then there are those who, when the national unemployment rate is low, say that this low rate demonstrates the effectiveness of fiscal policy; but when unemployment is high, this state of af-

---

1. The principal exclusion is the Neighborhood Youth Corps; most of the programs under this agency have only a minimal training component, and the summer programs offer scarcely any training at all.

fairs is cited as evidence of the failure of manpower training. I suggest to you that one important reason why we have had so much confusion and ineffectiveness in employment policy during the past decade is that too many policy makers have devoted themselves to advocacy rather than to analysis. Now I don't object to advocacy, per se; but I think that instead of displacing analysis it should allow and be based upon analysis.

Any reasonable evaluation of the overall effectiveness of manpower programs must begin with a recognition of their quite limited scope and size. With regard to size, we have probably never had more than about one slot for each fifteen or twenty eligible people. The Emergency Employment Act has provided one slot for each twenty-five or thirty of those eligible. We need more general recognition of this limitation and, I think, of the limited but nevertheless important role that manpower programs can play in society. It is important to understand that by themselves programs of this kind cannot cure unemployment; neither can they cure the welfare problem or the poverty problem. Each one of these problems is very tough, with roots deep in workings of our economic system. Any relatively superficial program, such as manpower training, will have some ameliorative effects; it will benefit some individual, as the findings of the studies that we have made thus far prove reasonably clearly. But it is wholly unreasonable, I think, to expect programs of this kind all by themselves to solve these problems that have been with us for so many years and that have resisted so many kinds of efforts to solve them.

Proper Role of Manpower Programs in Overall Policy

The real solutions of these problems must lie in some substantial structural changes in our economy, such as some basic modifications in the patterns of income distribution in the United States. We've been at that kind of game for many years now; there's nothing really radical about it, although after last year's presidential campaign it sounds radical. No doubt it is rather futile at this point to be talking about redistribution or even tax reform. But this country will come back to that issue. Until we face it, and until we make some progress on that and on some other kinds of structural change in the economy, I don't think that we can reasonably expect any substantial progress toward elimination of these overlapping problems of unemployment and welfare and poverty. But even these structural changes by themselves will not solve the problems we are talking about. You know, we Americans are very fond of the simple answer to the hard problem. We've got plenty of hard problems, and we apparently must learn over and over again that very few simple answers really work.

In this area particularly, it's important to remember a principle that some of our scientists have been emphasizing—the principle of synergism. Just as there are some drugs which in combination have a more powerful effect than the sum of each drug separately, so in the social field some programs work together; each strengthens the other's effect. I have used the analogy of the blades of a pair of scissors. You can accomplish much more with two blades of a pair of scissors than with only one. I think that principle applies to fiscal and monetary policy, to manpower programs, to job creation programs, as well as to these more fundamental structural changes. They all have to be blended together. The real problem is, what are the correct proportions? Too often we have had single-minded advocacy of one program or another which is offered as the ultimate answer to this or that problem. I'm a little sensitive on that point. I've been accused—very unjustly, I assure you—of promoting manpower programs at the expense of fiscal policy. The truth is that I have always emphasized both as essential components of an adequate employment policy. I have complained before, as I have tonight, that we have not devoted sufficient resources to manpower programs. But I have never argued that larger manpower programs would eliminate the need for fiscal policies aimed at the promotion of full employment. On the other hand, I could name for you certain economists who have contended that "pure and simple" fiscal policy, all by itself, could achieve full employment. I believe that our recent history, properly analyzed, refutes that contention.

If manpower programs are indeed sharply reduced in the near future, I don't believe that this will be the end of the matter. If such programs were eliminated completely by tomorrow morning, the national unemployment rate would immediately rise and reach a level of 6 percent, rather than the 5.2 percent currently reported. This would occur because most of the enrollees in these programs are officially counted as employed rather than as unemployed. In addition, there is a real possibility that we are approaching the peak of the present business cycle. Despite our high unemployment rate, economic activity generally is growing at an unsustainably high pace. There are some signs of overheating and there is talk of tightening monetary policy. Certainly President Nixon is striving to tighten fiscal policy. There are indications that sometime in the next twelve to eighteen months we may move into another recession. And another recession will mean, of course, a further rise—one of at least a full percentage point and probably more—in the unemployment rate.

Discussion of the alleged effects of the 1964 tax cut demonstrated the popularity of *post hoc ergo propter hoc* reasoning among economists generally and particularly among those in Washington. So, if manpower programs are eliminated or greatly reduced in size in 1973 and we then get an unemployment rate of 7 or 8 percent in 1974, there will surely be those who will say, "See what you did; you've knocked out manpower programs, so your unemployment rate is headed for the sky. We'd better get them back quickly." Unfortunately, so far as economic analysis in Washington is concerned, this kind of superficiality would be far from unprecedented.

Over the longer pull, I am confident that we will reach a more sensible evaluation of the proper role of manpower programs in an overall employment policy. I think we will come to see that no one of these programs—training, job-creation, fiscal-monetary innovation—is enough by itself, that each does strengthen the effect of the other, and that we must keep striving to find the best proportions in order to control excessive unemployment, which continues to be one of the great scourges of modern civilization.

THE INTEGRATION OF HIGHER EDUCATION INTO THE WAGE-LABOR SYSTEM

SAMUEL BOWLES

From Ivory Tower to Service Station

At least there is tolerably general agreement about what a university is not. It is not a place of professional education. Universities are not intended to teach the knowledge required to fit men for some special mode of gaining their livelihood.
—J. S. Mill

More knowledge has resulted from and led to service [by the university] for government and industry and agriculture. . . . All of this is natural. None of it can be reversed. . . . The campus has evolved consistently with society. . . . The university and segments of industry are becoming more and more alike. . . . The two worlds are merging. . . .
—Clark Kerr

The appearance of a radical student movement and the organization of radical professional and other white-collar workers in the late 1960s and early 1970s raise important questions. Will this radicalism among the highly educated play an important role in bringing about revolutionary changes in U.S. society? Or will unemployment and job insecurity among college graduates, along with the financial crisis of higher education, discipline young people to accept—if begrudgingly—the contours of U.S. society more or less as they are? Is the recent relative quiet of the cam-

NOTE: This paper grew out of discussions with Herbert Gintis and owes much to his "The New Working Class and Revolutionary Youth," *Review of Radical Political Economics*, II, No. 2 (Summer, 1970). I have benefited from the comments of many friends; from John Judis, Eli Zaretsky, Margaret Levi, Kieth Aufhauser, and Bill Lazonick, and particularly from the members of the Union of Radical Political Economics seminar at Harvard. An unabridged version is to appear in the *Review of Radical Political Economics*, V (1973). This version is printed here with the permission of the *Review*.

puses a sign that the movement has been assimilated, bought off, isolated, or destroyed? Or will it reappear, grow, and coalesce with radical movements among women, blacks, and workers in other sectors of the society?

Answers to these questions will be sought in an analysis of the economic and social forces underlying the movement. I will argue that the student movement and radicalism among young white-collar workers and professionals are a manifestation of structural weaknesses endemic to the corporate capitalist system and that the continuing evolution of the capitalist system will exacerbate these weaknesses and thus help to create the opportunity for radical change in the United States.

Central to my argument is the new political and economic importance of colleges and universities. Two hundred years ago the college was an elite cultural community on the periphery of the social and economic mainstream.

The growth of enrollments in higher education and the growth of the economy have been highly complementary developments, contributing both to each other and to the capacity of the educational system simultaneously to reproduce and legitimize the social relations of production and their manifestation in the system of social status stratification. Rapid growth of college enrollments, however, might have posed two difficult problems. First, increasing admissions to higher education would seem to necessitate greater equality of access. That this has not been the case is amply demonstrated by census data indicating that as the fraction of each age cohort attending college has increased there has been no reduction in the extent to which graduation from higher education depends upon the social status of one's family. A second possible problem posed by the flooding of the labor market with college graduates, a result of increased enrollments, is the necessity to maintain the monetary payoff for higher education without depressing the earnings of less-educated workers. Educational growth without economic growth would have required a lowering of the earnings of at least one category of workers. If increasing enrollments had implied a falling monetary payoff for higher education, discontent among students and their families would have been difficult to avoid, and the illusion of intergenerational betterment through increased schooling would have been lost. The political ramifications of imposing the necessary income losses on less-educated workers would have been equally unsettling. Yet census data for the last three decades indicate that the monetary payoff for a four-year college education has not suffered; nor have the earnings of other groups been lowered.

At Harvard, Yale, William and Mary, and a few others 200 years ago, some—but by no means all—of those who would enter the learned professions were trained and certified. The tradition of classical scholarship was maintained. And even among the economic elite of the day college attendance was the exception rather than the rule, a cultural luxury more than an economic or social necessity. In fact, no part of the formal educational system, not even elementary education, was particularly central to the process by which the economic order was reproduced and extended.

Higher education in the United States has come a long way in two centuries. Half of the relevant age group now attend post-secondary educational institutions. Colleges and universities have come to play a crucial part in the production of labor, in the reproduction of the class structure, and in the perpetuation and emendation of the dominant values and ideologies of the social order.

Higher education has taken its place alongside other types of schooling and the family as part of the process by which the corporate capitalist labor force is reproduced. Higher education has been integrated into the wage-labor system. This fact is of the utmost importance, for it bids us broaden our theoretical perspective on the sources and processes of social change and on the nature of contradiction in the capitalist system.

In this essay, I will formulate both a description and a theoretical interpretation of the ways in which the contradictory developments of the forces of production and the relations of production are manifested in the evolution of higher education in the United States. I hope that this analysis will provide a useful framework for the development of strategies for radical social change.

In the second section of this paper (condensed from a longer version), I will trace the historical role of schooling in ameliorating and depoliticizing the class conflicts associated with the accumulation of capital and the extension of the wage-labor system. In addition, I will discuss the ways in which the present structure of higher education operates to reproduce the class structure of the United States. In the third section, I will survey the recent evolution of the social relations of production in the U.S. economy and the accommodation to these changes in the transformation of the structure and content of higher education. In the fourth section, I will explore the ways in which these changes impinge on student life and argue that the strains associated with the transformation of higher education are manifestations of fundamental contradictions that have their origin in the structure of the corporate capitalist economy. The concluding section analyzes the student response—at once radical and backward-looking—and assesses the possibilities for radical change.

The Social Functions of Higher Education

> I have never considered mere knowledge ... as the only advantage derived from a good ... education. ... [Workers with more education] are more orderly and respectful in their deportment, and more ready to comply with the wholesome and necessary regulations of an establishment.... In times of agitation I have always looked to the most intelligent, best educated, and the most moral for support. The ignorant and uneducated I have generally found the most turbulent and troublesome, acting under the impulse of excited passion and jealousy.
>
> —*A Lowell, Mass., textile manufacturer writing to Horace Mann, Secretary of the Massachusetts Board of Education, 1841.*

Capital accumulation has been a driving force behind the transformation and growth of the U.S. economy. Living labor is combined in production with increasing amounts of past labor—in the form of schooling and training as well as machinery and other equipment. Two important aspects of the process of capital accumulation may be identified. The first is an expansion of the forces of production—the productive capacities of the economy—with a consequent rapid and sustained increase in the output of goods and services per worker. The second is an equally dramatic transformation of the social relations of production, manifested in the reduction of ever-increasing segments of the U.S. population to the status of wage labor. By the social relations of production, I mean the rules of authority among those engaged in production, the system of control over the work process, and the relations of property that govern the ownership of the product. The continued proletarianization of the U.S. labor force—which may be considered the other side of the ever-rising Gross National Product coin—has not been a placid process of gradual accommodation to economic progress. Workers, at least since the 1840s, have fought to retain control over their labor and its products.

The structure of U.S. education evolved in response to political and economic struggles associated with this process of capital accumulation and with the extension of a structure of production—the wage-labor system—in which the vast majority of workers surrender control over their labor in return for wages or salaries. The main periods of educational expansion and reform were coincident with the integration of major groups of workers into the wage-labor system and were a response by the capitalist class to the political and economic conflicts arising from this continued expansion of capitalist production relations. Thus, the two decades prior to the Civil War, which saw the rapid extension of public primary education and the consolidation of schools, were also a period of labor militancy associated with the rise of the factory system and the degradation of the worker. The progressive education movement, spanning the period from the 1890s to the 1920s, can be seen as a response to conflicts associated with the integration of peasant labor, both immigrant and native, into the burgeoning corporate-capitalist relations of production.

The modern U.S. educational system thus had its origins in the need of the capitalist class to ameliorate class conflict and obscure class interests in order to facilitate the uninterrupted accumulation of capital and the extension of the wage-labor system. The recent political conflict and impetus for reform in U.S. colleges and universities are hardly unprecedented; indeed, they are merely the manifestation at a higher level of forces which earlier propelled the history of U.S. education at the elementary and secondary levels. A crucial force behind the current ferment, I argue, is the continuing proletarianization of white-collar and previously self-employed labor, which has brought both student expectations and the structure of U.S. higher education into conflict with the social relations of production of the corporate-capitalist economy.

The particular intensity of recent conflict and reform efforts in U.S. education is a response to the integration of two major groups into the wage-labor system: uprooted Southern blacks and the once-respectable, "solid" members of the pre-corporate—capitalist community—the small-business people, the independent professionals, and other white-collar workers. Both groups have made an impact on education—the first mainly in elementary and secondary education, the latter chiefly in higher education. The expansion of the wage-labor system has also had an impact on the position of women and on the family. An important impetus for the current women's movement can be found in the integration of women into the wage-labor system and the penetration of commodity relations to the core of family life as more and more "household services" are bought and sold on the market. The historical coincidence of the integration into the wage-labor system of these three groups—women, blacks, and previously independent nonmanual workers—and the confluence of political movements associated with the process are a reflection of the law of uneven development. The fact that all these groups are undergoing a similar process, but from very different starting points, presents at once a great opportunity and challenge to radicals: How can the disparate consciousnesses of these three groups be brought together in an anticapitalist coalition that can work together with other potentially revolutionary groups? A theory and description adequate to our political needs would, of course, require a unified treatment of women, blacks, students, white-collar workers, younger or blue-collar workers, and others. The objective of this paper is more modest. I will dwell primarily on the political opportunities associated with the proletarianization of the previously independent white-collar group.

Assessing the political implication of the contradictions between the corporate-capitalist economy and the educational system requires an understanding of the two major social functions of higher education; namely, the reproduction of the social relations of producing and the expansion of the forces of production. The social relations of production are reproduced by equipping workers, technicians, and bosses alike with a set of skills, attitudes, and values that strengthens both the legitimacy of the hierarchical division of labor as a structure and each person's sense of deserving treatment within that structure. The social relations of production are reproduced in yet another sense: an individual's position in the hierarchical division of labor is to an important extent dependent upon the class position of his or her parents.

For the past century, at least, schooling has contributed to the reproduction of the social relations of production largely through the correspondence between school structure and class structure. Specifically, the social relations of education—the relations between students and teachers, students and students, and students and their work—replicate the social relations of production. The conditions of office or factory are reflected in the student's lack of control over his education, in the irrelevance of school work to the student's own interests, in the motivation of work by a system of grades and other external rewards rather than by the student's interest in either the process of production (learning) or the product (knowledge), in the persistent and ostensibly objective ranking and evaluation of students, in the emphasis on discipline and acceptance of authority, and in the supremacy of strict and unvaried routine. By attuning young people to a set of social relations similar to those of the work place, schooling teaches future workers not so much how to work as how to behave.

Moreover, the amount and kind of education received by each child are closely correlated with the position of his or her parents in the hierarchy of work relations. Those whose parents occupy subordinate positions in the production hierarchy are ordinarily enrolled in schools that lay heavy stress on the types of behavior required in those work roles: obedience and the ability to follow instructions. The sons and daughters of people holding positions of authority in the work hierarchy are usually educated in more "progressive" institutions—suburban high schools and liberal arts colleges, for example—which lay greater stress upon developing the student's ability to use information and to make independent decisions.

Thus, the educational system plays an important part in the intergenerational reproduction of the social relations of production.

The fact that colleges and universities have often been centers of radical discontent should not lead one to believe that higher education is an exception to these general principles. Like the rest of the school system, higher education has aided in the expansion of the productive capacities of the nation, the reproduction of the social class system, and the legitimation of the resulting inequalities.

Higher education in the United States has made a major contribution to economic growth. Recent economic development has depended heavily upon organizational and technical change—in short, upon the ability to devise new things to be produced and new ways to produce old things. Rapid technical and organizational change and the associated increase in output per capita have led to major shifts in the occupational structure. Particularly notable has been the rapid increase in the number of technicians and other white-collar workers—highly skilled and well educated but excluded from the central decision-making powers. Higher education has had a hand in the development of new technologies, both through the research sponsored at major universities and through the training of research personnel to work for private firms or for the government. Equally important, higher education has been a major producer of labor—labor with the skills and attitudes appropriate to the new methods of production and the changed occupational structure. Higher education is the last stage of the long process of socialization and training for those who will move into positions of authority or expertise in the occupational hierarchy of our society. It has been called the most complex initiation rite ever devised, but it is not simply a labeling ceremony. A college education contributes to a person's future income, in part through the knowledge gained in college. Of equal or greater importance are the patterns of behavior and the attitudes toward work, toward one's fellow workers, and toward authority that are inculcated in college. It is these attitudes and behavior patterns, more than the cognitive skills acquired in college, that facilitate the entrance of college graduates into the upper levels of the hierarchy of work relations.

The fact that, until recently, students in higher education were destined for relatively similar positions at the top of the occupational hierarchy allowed colleges and universities to perform this socializing function through the imposition of a set of rules or procedures that effectively prepared students for positions of power in business, the professions, and government. The social relations of the colleges reflected the social relations of production into which the students would enter in their adult life. There were few rules, and most of them could be got around; a wide choice of courses and majors was offered; the student was trained to exercise a considerable amount of independent discretion, as well as authority over much of his or her own affairs.

Thus, the social relations of college education have helped to produce graduates capable of the effective exercise of authority in large organizations. At the same time, the content of the curriculum has been geared to the production of graduates with the specialized knowledge and skills needed in the performance of the high-level bureaucratic and technical roles into which college graduates move.

But it is not merely through its contribution to the forces of production that higher education has served to maintain existing social institutions. It has also played a direct role in the reproduction of the social relations of production.

Whatever determined the occupational success of the older generation of the corporate elite—inherited wealth, nepotism, ability, theft, political power, or ambition—it is clear that, in order to reproduce this success, the next generation is virtually required to obtain a college degree. This reproduction of class standing has been facilitated, to a remarkable extent, through unequal access to higher education. Although the class position of parents is only weakly approximated by their income level or other measures of social status, such as educational level or occupation, some notion of the extent of differential class access to higher education can be gained from the following data: According to U.S. Census data for the late 1960s, even among those who had graduated from high school, children of families earning less than $3,000 per year were over six times as likely *not* to attend college as were the children of families earning over $15,000. Children from poorer families were also much less likely to graduate from high school; and, for those who did attend college, much more likely to enroll at the inexpensive, less prestigious colleges, particularly two-year rather than four-year institutions.

Access to higher education by a limited number of children of working-class families has served a number of important functions. It has lent credence to the myth of equal opportunity. At the same time, it has allowed the recruitment of new talent for the positions of power or expertise in the occupational hierarchy. Last, by allowing some aggressive and able working-class children to make it, it has provided a safety valve for the class system and, thus, served to drain off potential leadership from the working class.

Higher education in the United States has served not only to reproduce the class structure but to justify it. The fact that inequalities in educational credentials "fairly" gained have been added on to inequalities of class background has served to hide the importance of class itself in getting ahead. And, because higher education has ostensibly been open to all and promotion within the educational system has appeared to depend solely on one's own achievements, those who are successful tend to be seen as deserving. Partly for this reason, the bitterness arising from one's job or one's income or status is often directed against oneself rather than against the social system or those whose success was faciliated—if not predetermined—by that system. Radical thrusts against the dominant groups in society are blunted by the sentiment that "it's only fair; they have the education to do the job." By this same line of reasoning, poverty is often blamed on the poor: They are referred to as the "economically weak," not as the exploited.

Successful completion of higher education has thus come to confer a modern form of "right to rule" which is at least as persuasive and politically invulnerable as any of its divine, aristocratic, or plutocratic predecessors.

The growth of higher education itself has offered in people's daily experiences apparent verification of the myth. Because of the rapid growth of education at all levels, children are almost certain to attend school for a significantly longer period than their mothers and fathers did and so are likely to achieve a level of schooling that, in their parents' day, would have ensured high status and a good job. Thus, the educational system appears to be open and to sponsor a significant amount of mobility.

Quite apart from its role in verifying the myth of equal opportunity, college expansion, like the growth of per capita income, has helped to legitimize the capitalist system by demonstrating its capacity continually to produce more of everything. For many parents who themselves did not make it, the rapid growth of higher education has offered the satisfaction of having been able to provide well for their children.

Proletarianization of White-Collar Labor, Vocationalization of Higher Education

> If we can no longer keep the floodgates closed at the admissions office, it at least seems wise to channel the general flow away from four-year colleges and toward two-year extensions of high school in the junior and community colleges.
> —Amital Etzioni, Wall Street Journal, *March 17, 1970*

Continued capital accumulation and economic growth have provided the basis for a rapidly expanding system of higher education; they have also drastically altered the relationship of the educational system to the economy. The rapidly changing social relations of production under corporate capitalism has had two facets: the self-employed have become increasingly peripheral to the economy, and, at the same time, entire new cadres—technical and lower supervisory workers—have come to occupy a central role in the production system. Recent changes in U.S. higher education are an accommodation to these trends.

The expansion of capital, largely through accumulation by large corporations, has continued the integration of workers into the wage-labor system. Over the past century, the proportion of self-employed professionals and entrepreneurs to all economically active individuals has fallen from about two-fifths to less than a tenth; the relative numbers of salaried managers and professionals have multiplied by a factor of seven. And the relative number of wage earners has continued its steady rise. But these gross occupational categories obscure as much as they reveal. The nature of the labor process within occupations has been changing too. Work tasks have become more fragmented, the mental processes associated with them more specialized, and the social relations defined by work roles more limiting. Even in many well-paid, high-status jobs, the worker's discretion is increasingly limited.

The case of teaching provides a good example. It is easy to imagine teaching as relatively integrated, unalienated labor. The teacher is in direct contact with his or her material and has at least a modicum of control over his or her work; given a sufficiently vivid imagination, he or she may even entertain illusions of social usefulness. However, the teacher's job has undergone subtle change. The educational efficiency binge of the 1920s led to the application of business management methods to the high schools. The concentration of decision-making power in the hands of administrators and the quest for economic rationalization had the same disastrous consequences for teachers that bureaucracy and rationalization of production had on most other workers. In the interests of so-called scientific management, control of curriculum, evaluation, counseling, even of texts, and teaching methods was placed in the hands of "experts." A host of specialists arose to deal with minute fragments of the teaching job. The tasks of thinking, making decisions, and understanding the goals of education were placed in the hands of educational experts and bureaucrats.

Ostensibly to facilitate administration and reap economies of large-scale production, schools became larger and more impersonal. The possibility of intimate or complicated classroom relationships gave way to the social relations of the production line.

The fragmentation of tasks and the demise of intimate personal contact has not been limited to teaching but, rather, has pervaded all the service professions. The medical sector, for example, has seen the rise of large, impersonal medical bureaucracies, the ascendancy of specialists, and the demise of the general practitioner, who once ministered to the health of the whole body and the whole family.

Along with the virtual demise of the self-employed worker and the integration of white-collar labor into fragmented and hierarchically stratified work roles, the expansion of corporate capital has brought the rapid development of new kinds of skilled, subprofessional workers. The new cadres include technicians, lower-level supervisory personnel, secretaries, nonretail sales workers, dental assistants, draughtsmen, and paraprofessional personnel in medicine and education, to name just a few of the rapidly growing occupational titles.

The rapid growth in college enrollments has been in part a response to the needs generated by this changing occupational structure, and this expansion has, in turn, brought about two important changes in the social position of higher education. First is the increasing scientific, cultural, and social importance of the college community. Second is the frank recognition that some colleges have become the training ground for much more than the economic elite; community colleges and many four-year institutions have taken up the task of training the middle-level bureaucrats and technicians of the future. While the adaptation to both of these consequences of growth has, for the most part, preserved the fundamental functions of higher education, the adjustments are far from perfect and have revealed some of the underlying weaknesses of the corporate-capitalist system. In the remainder of this section, I will argue, first, that the culture of the college community is anachronistic and dysfunctional, given its now greatly enlarged clientele, and, second, that the community-college movement may be seen as only a partly successful attempt to deal with some of the unsettling consequences of the increasing diversity of socialization functions that have been imposed on higher education by the increasing enrollments.

Over a century ago, Marx (in *Capital,* Vol. I) foresaw that the continued expansion of the forces of production under capitalism might necessitate the development of a labor force whose skills and outlook would bring it into conflict with the social relations of production.

> Modern industry compels society . . . to replace the detail worker of today, crippled by life-long repetition of one and the same trivial operation, and thus reduced to the mere fragment of a man, by the fully developed individual, fit for a variety of labors ready to face any change in production and to whom the different social functions he performs are but so many modes of giving free scope to his own natural and acquired powers.

But will such a labor force acquiesce in the social relations of corporate-capitalist production? André Gorz expresses the problem succinctly:

> The problem for big management is to harmonize two contradictory necessities: the necessity of developing human capabilities, imposed by modern processes of production, and the political necessity of ensuring that this kind of development of capabilities does not bring in its wake any augmentation of the independence of the individual, provoking him to challenge the present division of social labor and distribution of power.

As long as the vast proportion of college students was destined for positions of leadership, the tradition of scholarship and unfettered inquiry was probably an appropriate context for college training. Yet, with over half of each age cohort continuing schooling after high school, it is clear that both leaders and followers are being trained. The educational processes best suited to training an elite may be less successful in fostering quiescence among followers. Incompatibility of functions seems certain to arise as higher education is forced to combine the teaching of intellectual skills with an increased role in the perpetuation of a conservative social mythology and the socialization of docility among middle-level workers. Moreover, the contradictions of the larger society increasingly impinge on the classroom. The struggles of blacks, women, Third World people, welfare recipients, and others have starkly revealed the seamy side of American reality and are rapidly serving to explode the legitimating ideologies taught in our colleges and high schools.

The political ramifications of a failure to adapt the culture and objectives of the university community to its new diversity of social functions are fairly obvious. The economic consequences are no less important. Skilled and professional labor power, like all labor power, is embodied in people. The process of embodiment—training and education—is time-consuming and, for good economic reasons, is undertaken at a young age, in large measure in specialized institutions—schools, colleges, and other training institutions. But skills are not learned in a vacuum. Because of the cultural environment of the traditional college community and the nature of many of the skills themselves, the educational process seems increasingly to provide the means but not the motivation to be a useful cog in the corporate-capitalist system. Moreover, the fact that high-paid skills and competence are embodied in workers—and, unlike capital, cannot be severed from them—provides an insurance against dire poverty and economic hardship and thus relieves some of the economic pressures that force less well-educated labor into the labor market at the mercy of employers.

As a result, there have been strong barriers to the development of a market in skills and ideas in which services flow readily to the highest bidder. Teachers, researchers, and other college graduates may increasingly impose qualitative as well as monetary conditions upon the rental of their services to business and government.

Recent tendencies in high-level teaching and research may be seen as only a partially successful attempt to deal with this problem. With the specialization of jobs in the economy has come a fragmentation of studies and research. Increasingly, no student, no researcher, is encouraged to deal with a whole problem, any more than a worker is allowed to produce a whole product. The artificial compartmentalization of intellectual pursuits allows the development of advanced technique within each area and simultaneously militates against the application of comprehensive moral standards or the consideration of the larger social consequences of one's work. The narrowing effect of academic specialization is furthered by the modern conception of professionalism in which the intellectual is seen as a technician whose success may be adequately judged by his skill in devising technical solutions to technical problems.

In addition, the research functions of the intellectual community are increasingly severed from their university base, to be carried out in large private or government laboratories and institutes where the cultural climate is more favorable.

But these strategies are met with resistance from all sides. Researchers ordinarily prefer to be associated with a university, partly for reasons of status emanating from the peculiar culture of intellectuals and partly to maintain easy access to graduate students and the broader scientific community. Far more important, students at both the graduate and undergraduate levels increasingly reject specialization and "professionalism," demanding, instead, multidisciplinary approaches to whole problems.

The increasingly vocational orientation of intellectual pursuits fostered by today's colleges is but one outgrowth of the conflict between the traditional elite-training function of the university and the greatly expanded numbers of students enrolled. Another is the growth of two-year colleges and post-secondary technical institutes, a manifestation of the impossibility of accommodating half of each age cohort in elite institutions. The booming community-college movement has created a class stratification within higher education parallel to the hierarchical relations of production in the modern corporation. An expansion of the number of students in higher education has thus been made possible without undermining the elite status and function of the established institutions.

With a small fraction of each age group attending college, most students could be accommodated at four-year institutions, graduation from which virtually ensured future economic and social success. Of course, there were always institutions that could not automatically confer status, but these were confined largely to a few fields (such as education and divinity) and to the South (particularly black colleges).

The idea that those who had made it into college had made it to the top did not survive the tremendous increase in enrollments. But it is not merely the expectation of success that has to change; the entire structure of higher education has become inadequate. A relatively uniform system of higher education enrolling so large a fraction of each age group would fail in a number of ways. The right to rule and the expectation of privilege would be extended to social groups that, in their jobs and their political activities, had previously exercised very little influence over their own lives or those of others. Unrealistic occupational and status expectations would be encouraged in working-class children; disappointment would undoubtedly result in discontent. Equally important, the social relations of the educational process itself—based on the notion that the colleges and universities were socializing an elite—would prove inappropriate when these institutions began training middle-level workers. Thus, a uniform system of higher education would foster discontent and competition for power, for it would legitimize the aspirations for power and wealth among much more than the old elite, and it would fail to inspire the expectations and submissiveness appropriate to the future work roles of most of the newcomers to postsecondary schooling.

Structural change in educational processes has thus been necessitated by two parallel movements: growth in enrollments and continuing change in the social relations of production, manifested in the fragmentation and routinization, in short, in the prolitarianization, of white-collar labor. The 1960s and 1970s thus present many parallels to the period around the turn of the present century, which saw the expansion of secondary education as a means of integrating peasant and working-class children into the wage-labor system.

The repetition in our colleges and universities of the high school expansion and stratification process has been under way for some time and for similar reasons. Concerns about poverty and racial discrimination and the desire to placate previously excluded middle- and lower-income families have given increased impetus to the movement.

Enrollments in community colleges are over three times what they were ten years ago and include by far the most rapidly growing body of college students. Higher education has developed a multitiered system, dominated at the top by the Ivy League institutions and the great state universities, followed by the state colleges, and ending with the community colleges. This system reflects both the social-status structure of the families of the students and the hierarchy of work relations into which the various types of students will move after graduation.

The results of a recent study of one of the more egalitarian systems—California's—illustrate this stratified system. Over 18 percent of the students at the University of California in the mid-1960s came from families earning $20,000 or more, while fewer than 7 percent of the students in community colleges (and fewer than 4 percent of the youth who were *not* receiving higher education) came from such families. Similarly, while only 12.5 percent of the students attending the University of California came from families earning less than $6,000, 24 percent of those attending community colleges and 32 percent of the youth not enrolled in higher education came from such families.

The segregation of students not destined for the top has allowed the development of procedures and curricula more appropriate to their future needs as defined by their actual occupational opportunities. The vast majority of students in community colleges are programed for failure, and great efforts are made—through testing and counseling—to convince students that their lack of success is objectively attributable to their own inadequacies. The process of bringing student hopes into line with the realities of the job market is facilitated by a tracking system within the community college much like the channeling system of high schools, with four-year-college transfer programs for the "promising" and vocational programs for the "dead-enders." The magnitude of the task of lowering student expectations can hardly be exaggerated, for at least three times as many entering community-college students want to complete four or more years of college as actually succeed in doing so. Fewer than half of community-college entrants receive even the two-year Associate of Arts degree. For those who stay, studies at community colleges are, much more than in four-year colleges, explicitly vocational, emphasizing such middle-level goals as training in nursing, computer work, and office skills. The connection between the needs of business and the curricula of community colleges is fostered by business representation on advisory boards. The continuing vocationalization of the community-college curriculum is now actively being pushed by the business community, the federal government, and major private foundations, particularly the Carnegie Corporation.

The needs of the corporate elite are also reflected in the social relations of education at the community colleges. The student is allowed little discretion in selecting courses. Systems of discipline and student management resemble those of secondary education more than those of the elite universities; these colleges have been called "high schools with ashtrays." The teaching staff is recruited heavily from the corps of high school teachers. State legislatures exert pressure to increase teaching loads and class sizes and, in some cases, even to standardize curriculum and teaching methods. The social relations of the community-college classroom increasingly resemble the formal, hierarchical impersonality of the office or the uniform processing of the production line.

All this, of course, must be seen not as a failure of the community-college movement but, rather, as a successful adaptation to the tasks they were set up to perform; processing large numbers of students to attain that peculiar combination of technical competence and social acquiescence required in the skilled but powerless upper-middle positions in the occupational hierarchy of the corporate capitalist economy.

The vocational orientation of the community colleges is becoming more typical of U.S. higher education as a whole. This process is in large part a result of the rapid increase in the proportion of all college students who are enrolled in community colleges. Nor is this proportion likely to level off. Current projections are for the community-college enrollment to continue its rapid rise while total enrollment in all colleges slowly moves toward a plateau in the late 1970s or early 1980s. Four-year institutions thus stand to *lose* enrollments over the next decade. Moreover, the four-year institutions are likely to come under pressure for a "rationalization" of curriculum and educational method as the financial crisis of the colleges and universities intensifies. State legislatures and other funding bodies are already pushing for more job-relevant curricula, heavier teaching loads, and more teacher accountability at the four-year institutions.

The Expansion of Corporate Capital and Contradictions of Student Life

> We refuse to buy the right not to die of hunger by running the risk of dying of boredom!
> —*Student slogan, Paris, May 1968*

Student life has been radically changed by the transformation of higher education. The rapid increase in enrollments over the past half-century, the central role of university research and personnel in the domestic and international expansion of corporate capital, the social stratification of higher education, the vocationalization of the curriculum, the rationalization of methods in order to process more students more cheaply—all these changes have impinged on students' daily experience. The process of change, though carefully engineered by university administrators and adroitly sold by apologists for the new order, has not been placid. Since the Berkeley uprising of the early 1960s, students in revolt against mechanized, mass-produced education have announced that they will not be folded, spindled, or mutilated. Attempts to relate the college community more directly to service to the state and the business community are met with ever more direct resistance. Attacks on ROTC and other war-related establishments on campus have been widespread. The protest has extended to graduate students and young professionals. Dozens of radical professional organizations have sprung up, in medicine, sociology, the physical sciences, economics, psychiatry, engineering, law, city planning, and Asian, African, and Latin American studies, to mention just a few. These groups give tangible political expression to a growing conviction among students, young teachers, and other professionals that their function is not to administer society but to change it drastically. Dr. Edward Teller's recent assessment of the strength of the movement was clearly extravagant but heartening nonetheless. He told a Presidential commission that events in universities in 1969 and 1970 had "practically cut the connection between universities and defense related industries. . . . In twenty years," he warned, "the U.S. will be disarmed."

At least during full-employment periods, campus recruiters for big business and the government find a cooler reception than in the past. Direct political action, which was originally focused against companies in the war business, is now aimed at a much broader range of targets—General Motors, General Electric, Polaroid, and the Peace Corps, for example. Student attacks on campus recruitment by the U.S. Information Service, Department of State, and companies with substantial international operations are indications of the repugnance felt by many students at being trained to administer the U.S. world empire.

Assaults against the multitiered educational stratification system, pressures for open enrollment, and (among students already enrolled) demands for access to prestigious institutions have mounted. In New York City, black and Puerto Rican students took the lead in "opening up" the previously highly selective city colleges. In Seattle and elsewhere, minority students have resisted being shunted into the newly formed vocational tracks at the bottom of the educational pyramid. Lagging attendance in specifically vocational programs has reflected a hostility, or at least massive indifference, to these curriculums. Across the country, women and blacks are demanding, not middle-level vocational skills, but an education that can help to fight sexism and racism.

Other responses have been less political. Some decide not to go to college at all. Some drop out. Many go and stay but turn on to drugs and turn off from intellectual and political pursuits.

Thus, the integration of U.S. higher education into the wage-labor system has produced political strain and a deep-seated malaise, which persist even during periods when an uneasy calm prevails on most campuses. For what we are witnessing is not the growing pains of a healthy organism but, rather, the manifestations of fundamental contradictions in the larger society.

The nature of the contradiction may be briefly summarized. The expansion of enrollments, like the expansion of capital, continues to be essential in legitimizing the class structure and allowing its reproduction from generation to generation. Yet the material well-being and transformed social relations of production induced by the expansion of capital have produced an incongruence between the aspirations of college students, on the one hand, and the manpower requirements of the economy, on the other. In short, colleges can no longer make good their promises. Most students are simply not getting enough of what they want out of higher education. To the extent that students see college as an investment in a better job, three broad types of objectives may be identified: money, status, and rewarding work. Of the three, the expectation of a monetary payoff is the most likely to be fulfilled, at least for the minority who manage to receive a four-year degree. That a college degree continues to be an investment which pays well no doubt helps to explain the hold colleges continue to exercise on the public imagination. But increasingly students, particularly the more affluent ones, see their education as a means of access to rewarding work. Desirable jobs are coming to be regarded as those that contribute to social betterment or are an aid to the continuous development of one's creative, aesthetic, emotional, intellectual, and other capacities. Like the dispossessed artisans and farmers of the nineteenth century, students increasingly reject the fragmentation of tasks and the hierarchy of production in the modern corporation; they want to be their own bosses. Less affluent students often see further education as the route to respectability through access to a high-status job.

With the rapid expansion of higher education, with over half the age group continuing education beyond high school, there are simply not enough rewarding, high-status jobs to go around. The increasing discrepancy between jobs and expectations is no passing phenomenon. Both the change in student consciousness and the declining opportunities for rewarding and high-status work are firmly rooted in three aspects of the process of capitalist expansion—namely, in the level of material affluence, in the stratified and alienating social relations of production, and in the pervasiveness of waste and irrational production necessary to absorb the surplus productive capacity of the economy.

The ever-increasing level of material well-being—both that of the students' families and that which they reasonably expect to enjoy after they leave college— has reduced the urgency of immediate consumption needs. Thus, the success of the economic growth process has itself undermined much of the monetary rationale for getting a college degree; it has changed the way in which many students value the economic payoff to their studies. For many the calculation of monetary gain has become secondary to other aspects of education; the other job-related objectives—rewarding work and status—become primary. With the lure of the external monetary reward on the wane, students—particularly the more affluent—demand that education be intrinsically rewarding: College study must be interesting and enjoyable and must contribute to the individual's personal development.

The social relations of production under corporate capitalism represent a major obstacle to meeting student aspirations for either rewarding work or status. Alienated labor now characterizes most of the occupational slots open to college graduates. Most graduates now move into jobs in which they exercise little control over the disposition of their own labor power and neither own nor identify personally with the product of their labor. Thus, work tasks tend to be repetitive, fragmented, and meaningless. The time spent on the job is not only physically and emotionally draining, it is worse, for it stunts the individual's creative and personal development, channeling his energies into the development of those skills and capacities that are valued only insofar as they bring a little more job security or a slightly larger paycheck.

The social relations of production thwart the status aspirations of students as much as they obliterate the possibility of rewarding work. The continued expansion of corporate capital has altered the system of status differentiation. Many of the high-status occupations—the independent businessman, the self-employed professional—are losing numbers. The job vacancies open to people who have been to college are now found in the well-paying but lackluster middle rungs of the corporate hierarchy. Even without changes in the availability of high-status jobs, there would not be enough status to go around. The nature of the status objective itself—based, as it is, on invidious distinctions—makes it unattainable to most of the vast numbers of students now enrolled in two- and four-year institutions. The promise of high status seemingly offered by admission to community colleges is a particularly cruel hoax. The occupational opportunities and likely incomes of workers with less than four years of college fall far short of the opportunities open to graduates of four-year colleges. Four-year college graduates are over twice as likely to end up in the high-status professional or technical jobs as are those who have less than four years of college. Those without four-year degrees are over twice as likely to end up in clerical jobs. As of 1968, the difference in expected lifetime income between high-school graduates and four-year college graduates (as calculated by the U.S. Census Bureau) is $47,000; for those who have been to college for fewer than four years, the advantage over high-school graduates is a paltry $7,000.

The waste and irrationality that characterize production under corporate capitalism also limit the opportunities for rewarding work. The alienated white-collar worker lacks a personal identification with the product of his or her labor, not simply because the product is owned by the capitalist, but because, in many cases, the product does not meet any real human need. The product of work may be as alienating as the process. The ecology and consumer-protection movements, the pervasive demands for more adequate social services, and the Third World liberation movements have all helped to reveal the massive waste and irrationality of what is produced in the United States. To more and more young people, having a hand in producing it has little appeal. A growing number of such people, who feel that too many commodities for private consumption are produced already, balk at most work prospects available in a capitalist economy. Others, sensitive to concerns such as environmental issues, can feel nothing better than ambivalence about their work. And, while not long ago employment in military and war-related work was seen as a social contribution, now it is more often taken on with only a sense of humiliation, embarrassment, or even contempt. The new armies of workers involved in packaging, product design and redesign, advertising, and other aspects of the sales effort are face to face with the fact that the object of their labor is capitalists' profits, not the satisfaction of consumer needs. Even work in the production of education itself has lost much of its appeal. The smug ideology that once celebrated the enlightening and equalizing mission of the teaching profession has given way under the pressure of radical political movements and radical critiques to a more persuasive, though less inspiring, view of education, stressing its inegalitarian and repressive functions.

The uninviting job prospects for college students are thus a manifestation of contradictions in the evolving structure of the corporate capitalist economy. On the one hand, the expansion of corporate capital has provided much of the impetus for the increase in enrollment. On the other, the changing social relations of production and the growing waste and irrationality associated with corporate capitalist expansion have altered the structure of work so as to thwart student aspirations. Much of the student protest of the past decade has been a reflection of this basic contradiction. Student protest has its roots in other contradictions of the larger society as well. Attacks on campus racism arise less from the peculiarities of college life than from the nationwide movement for racial self-determination. The fight against ROTC and campus military recruiters is just a small part of the world-wide anti-imperialist struggle. Likewise, the radicalism of many young teachers, technicians, social workers, and other professionals is a response to the continuing failure to place the nation's productive capacities and fiscal resources in the service of the people.

Similarly, the fact that the political manifestations of the movement are confined largely to the campuses and the professional organizations should not obscure their broader social importance. The weakening of the reproductive role of higher education represents an opportunity for radical change, not only on the campuses, where the contradictions are now most acutely felt, but also in other sections of the society, where the crisis in higher education will help destroy the mythology of opportunity and progress and thus reveal the shortcomings of the social institutions regulating our lives.

Consequences of contradictory development: petty bourgeois consciousness and the revolutionary potential

> The tradition of all the dead generations weighs like a nightmare on the brain of the living. And just when they seem engaged in revolutionizing themselves and things, in creating something that has never yet existed, precisely in such periods of revolutionary crisis they anxiously conjure up the spirits of the past to their service and borrow from them names, battle cries and costumes, in order to present the new scene of world history in this time-honored disguise and this borrowed language.
> —K. Marx, *The Eighteenth Brumaire of Louis Bonaparte*

Like the nineteenth-century labor movement, the student movement today is in large measure a product of the proletarianization of labor that accompanies the accumulation of capital. Like the early labor movement, too, it has combined militant action and a sometimes radical rhetoric with a backward-looking consciousness.

The skilled factory hands who sought to regain the freedom they lost with the demise of craft production, the agricultural workers and farm tenants who bemoaned the bygone respectability and independence of the family farmer, find their twentieth-century echo in the college student who despises the thought of salaried work in the corporate bureaucracy and longs for the free-wheeling personal independence of the self-employed professional or owner-entrepreneur. The same backward-looking consciousness finds expression in the teachers or engineers who agonize at the loss of status and independence as they are absorbed into large bureaucracies.

The precapitalist Jeffersonian ideal—the small community of property owners—that captured the imagination of dispossessed farmers and craftsmen a century or more ago was gradually extinguished, for it had been bypassed by the growth of the competitive capitalist system. Today, the competitive capitalist ideal—the individuality and respectability of the individual entrepreneur or professional—is expressed in slightly altered form in students' definitions of a good job and in their desire to "do their own thing." Like the precapitalist Jeffersonian ideal, this competitive capitalist vision conflicts sharply with the reality of the corporate capitalist economy. The underlying aspirations which unify the student movement, contemporary youth culture, and the malaise of many young white-collar workers are thus a hip emendation of petty-bourgeois consciousness.

Unlike the nineteenth-century workers and farmers, whose precapitalist consciousness was often rooted in their own experience as independent producers, today's discontented students draw their backward-looking consciousness largely from their parents. The student values of independence, initiative, individuality, and social service reflect the often unrealized aspirations of a parental generation of independent craftsmen or professionals and small businessmen. These values were passed on to the younger generation through patterns of progressive child-rearing, as well as by more formal indoctrination. Well before the 1960s, the accumulation of corporate capital had undermined the economic basis of the parents' entrepreneurial values. The social relations of production of corporate capitalism had been radically transformed, leaving the parents of the college generation more often than not in wage or salary employment and drastically altering the occupational structure open to their children. The result was a massive discrepancy between the backward-looking consciousness of the college generation and the contemporary and future structure of jobs and work for which students were preparing.

Despite all the discontent that has been generated, the contradiction between the structure and growth of higher education, on the one hand, and the expansion of corporate capital, on the other, has thus not produced a revolutionary or socialist consciousness among students. Yet the contradictions underlying student protest are likely to intensify, for they are deeply rooted in the process of capitalist expansion. As the continued proletarianization of white-collar work continues to propel the vocationalization and stratification of U.S. higher education, the political expression of the contradictions in higher education may begin to take a more radical form. Two tendencies, though of seemingly minor importance at the present, are likely to manifest themselves in strength over the next decade.

First, by escalating serious class and racial inequalities from secondary to higher education, the expansion of enrollments has done much more than increase the awareness of the degree of inequality in our school system. It has created in the mass of nonelite college students a group of people who have had at least a taste of inequality and hardship, who are old enough to be politically active and yet young enough to have dreams and take chances, and who are brought together on a day-to-day basis through common experiences and, in some cases, common residence. No such potential political force could be found when the main work of social class selection was being done at the high school level. For until recently, at least, the high school students themselves were barely aware of what was being done to them and were perhaps too dependent on their elders to act. The parents, in turn, were both too busy providing for themselves and their children and too dispersed and unknown to each other to be a potent political force. Not surprisingly, only rarely did working-class and minority-group parents of high school students develop cohesive political movements with the staying power to engage in more than episodic struggles over the schooling of their children.

Campus political discontent outside the elite colleges may signal the beginning of a broad struggle for greater equality in higher education. Certainly events such as the strike at San Francisco State College in 1968 and the struggle for open enrollment have revealed the shortsighted and narrow limits within which the corporate elite and other privileged groups are willing to make concessions to Third World and less affluent students. These conflicts have thus helped to clarify the fundamental role of the community colleges and some state colleges in the class hierarchy of higher education, thereby undermining one of the central legitimizing beliefs of the capitalist order.

A second source of potential radicalization arises from parallel contradictions in U.S. higher education and in the evolution of the class structure. Until recently, professional workers and white-collar labor have smugly accepted the comforting view that they constituted a privileged group—a modern aristocracy of labor. They had greater job security, greater control over their work, and, of course, more money. They had little reason to be critical of the hierarchical social division of labor. Along with the substantially overlapping group of property owners, they were the main beneficiaries of the capitalist system, and they constituted the foundation of its political defense.

While the earnings of professional and other white-collar workers have continued to exceed those of blue-collar workers by a good margin, the resulting consumption privileges accruing to this labor elite have become increasingly unimportant for many. At the same time highly valued privileges in production have rapidly been withdrawn. The working conditions of office and "brain" labor have increasingly been coming to resemble those of the production line. The widespread unemployment and job insecurity of engineers, teachers, and technicians are symptomatic of these changes.

Although the labor force remains highly segmented by occupational level as well as by race and sex, the process of capital accumulation itself has greatly reduced the number of workers with a direct personal interest in the perpetuation of the social relations of corporate capitalist production. The concentration of capital and the demise of the small property-owning producer have narrowed the base of support for private ownership of the means of production. The concomitant decline in the number of workers exercising independence and control in their work has created a great mass of working people—now the overwhelming majority—who experience production as a social rather than an individual process, and who have little to lose and much to gain by the overthrow of the hierarchical division of labor in favor of collective control of production. The continued expansion of corporate capital may belatedly create a common condition of work among all segments of the labor force and thus provide the objective economic basis for a comprehensive working-class consciousness.

But consciousness does not change automatically in response to a changing economic reality. Much will depend on the objectives pursued by students, by organizations of young white-collar and professional workers, and by the groups with which they ally themselves. If they act out the retrospective consciousness of many students and other young people, if they seek to restore their lost privileges in the hierarchy of production—as independent decision makers and directors of the labor of others—they will isolate themselves from other workers. Attempts by teachers' unions to limit student or community power in the educational process provide a glaring example of strategies that reinforce rather than undermine the corporate-capitalist order. Similarly, if white-collar workers seek compensation for their lost autonomy and faded status in higher earnings, allies will be hard to come by. But if these goals, derived from looking backward, are rejected in favor of demands for a wider collective participation in control over production, the movement will find roots in a broad segment of the population. For it is possible that over the next decades workers in all occupational categories, as well as students, will increasingly trace their frustrations to a common set of obstacles barring their pursuit of rewarding work and a better life. The corporate capitalist economy—with its bias in favor of hierarchy, waste, and alienation in production, and its mandate for a school system attuned to the reproduction and legitimation of the associated hierarchical division of labor—may then be seen as a source of the problem.

As individual salvation through access to higher education is shown to be an empty promise, the appeal of political solutions will increase. With much of the legitimizing ideology of the capitalist system destroyed by everyday experience, the ground would be laid for a broad-based movement demanding participatory control of our productive and educational institutions and for the development of a liberating education and its complement, a humane and efficient social technology of production.

The contradictions of corporate capitalism will not, by themselves, create a revolutionary movement, but they do give birth to a revolutionary potential. The contradictions now manifest in higher education provide us with the opportunity to organize and to continue the uphill struggle to bring that revolutionary potential to fruition.

REFERENCES

Bowles, S. "Understanding Unequal Economic Opportunity, the Role of Schooling, I.Q., and Social-Class Background." *American Economic Review,* May 1973.

———. "Unequal Education and the Reproduction of the Social Division of Labor." *Review of Radical Political Economy,* III, No. 3 (Fall 1971).

———, and Gintis, H. "I.Q. in the U.S. Class Structure." *Social Policy,* Jan.-Feb., 1973.

Edwards, R.; Reich, M.; and Weisskopf, T. *The Capitalist System.* Englewood Cliffs, N.J.: Prentice-Hall, 1972.

Karabel, J. "Community Colleges and Social Stratification." *Harvard Educational Review,* Nov. 1972.

HOW MUCH AND WHAT KINDS OF EDUCATION FOR ECONOMIC DEVELOPMENT?

RICHARD ECKAUS

One of the great solutions to social and economic problems, according to the conventional folklore, is an educational system. And, according to the folklore, the nostrum works in both more-advanced and less-developed economies. Thus, the remedy for problems ranging from crime in the streets and racial prejudice in the United States to lack of development in the poor countries of the world is more and better education. If there is any qualification attached to this conventional wisdom it is that even if education is no panacea neither can it do any harm and it obviously must make the individuals who acquire it better off.

But education is not free. It absorbs resources. Providing more education requires allocating more resources to it. As the economist is continually pointing out, resources are always scarce; in the less-developed countries of the world they are particularly scarce. A decision to provide more education implies, therefore, a decision to have less of something else, at least in the short run.

To rely simply on the claims of folklore as to its general advantages is not a satisfactory way of making decisions about education. It is necessary to be as hardheaded and as careful as possible in thinking about the benefits which can be expected to flow from the expansion of the educational system and the costs which are entailed. It is necessary to expose the limitations of conventional dogmas and to inspect carefully the various techniques of economic analysis of education. Both aspects of the subject will be treated here, and on the basis of this analysis some final suggestions will be made with respect to methods of formulating educational policy for less-developed countries.

Sources of Difficulty in Making Educational Policy for Development

The first step is to identify the difficulties which are involved both in evaluating the conventional folklore and in improving educational policy making. These difficulties, which at present constrain our ability to make good educational decisions, can also be regarded as an agenda for research.

To start with, the term *education* is itself somewhat misleading. It stands for *learning,* and also, when used explicitly or implicitly with the word *system,* education can mean the particular formal institutions or schools which are created to accomplish learning. One of the major problems in making educational policy is that while we are really interested in learning we know relatively little about the relation between educational systems and learning. This is not the occasion on which to cite evidence, but consider the surprise which has greeted those studies in the United States which indicate that differences in the quality of the educational system are of limited significance for learning as conventionally measured and as revealed by test scores. This surprise suggests our lack of understanding of learning processes and how a formal educational system affects them.

The confession of ignorance about learning in educational systems should not offend professional teachers, particularly when it is recognized that, in spite of limited understanding of the learning process, many teachers are nonetheless obviously quite good at what they are doing.

A major difficulty in making educational policy for development is that *development* is also a term with a number of different meanings, reflecting, in part, the existence of a number of social goals in the whole development package and, in part, disagreement as to the relative weight which should be given to various goals.

All the different development goals can be classified either as output or equity objectives. Development is, perhaps, most commonly thought of in output terms: Improvement in the material conditions of life, the achievement of an overall growth rate, or some future target such as balance-of-payments equilibrium or self-sufficiency in particular products. The equity goals of development can mean many different things to different people: reduction in income inequality, reduction in unemployment, or specific policies such as land reform or a progressive income tax. Particular equity objectives, although they may not be generally agreed on, are important; controversy over them can bring down governments.

To an unusual degree, there is uncertainty about goals and methods of achieving them in the field of educational decision making. Yet decisions must be made. So the difficult problem which we must now face squarely is how to make decisions about education when there are somewhat conflicting goals and our knowledge about how to achieve them is limited.

Limitations of folklore and maxims

It is easier to identify the errors which have been made in assessing the relations between education, schooling, and economic development than to state what the correct relations are, which might be excuse enough for starting with the errors and exposing them before going on to the hard part. It is also instructive, however, to examine various rules which have been proposed and the methods which have been used in making educational policy in order to determine what can be learned from them.

Suppose we ask simply, "Why is education important for development?" The answer seems so transparently obvious that perhaps I should be ashamed to ask the question. Clearly if a country is to have agronomists to improve agricultural practices the country has to educate or import agronomists. Likewise, engineers are required for factories, doctors for hospitals, electronic technicians for radio and telephone networks, and so on. Not all can be imported. That means there must be an educational system.

But this conclusion does not help very much in making the essential budget decisions of how much and what kind of education. Are there minimum requirements for education which must be met or is the rule "the more the better?"

Suppose you did the following: On one side of a graph you put down average years of education, on the other side put down the national income per capita or standard of living or any other commonly used measure of economic development. Then locate each country on the chart. The United States has a high per capita income and a high level of education. India has a low level of income and a low level of schooling. Put every country on the chart. You will get a "scatter diagram" which will drift up from India to the United States. Higher levels of average income will be associated with higher levels of education. Doesn't that prove "the more the better?"

No! What the scatter diagram shows is that there is an association, not cause and effect. There are many other differences among the countries on the scatter diagram, and some of those rather than education may be the really critical differences. Even if the effect which education has on development is positive and causal, it may, in fact, be relatively slight. Moreover, it is possible, even likely, that when income rises people *demand* more education. So what we are observing in the scatter diagram may be a demand effect—a result, not a cause.

Shouldn't it be possible to separate cause and effect? It would be possible if more data were available and if we were smarter about the nature of the cause and effect relations and other influences on both education and income. Not having more data and being stuck at least for the present with our limited understanding, all we can say is that education and average income are associated.

What if we take into account the effects of education on the noneconomic goals of development? For such goals is it not clear with respect to education that "the more the better?" It is true that in many places there has been a decrease in racism, regionalism, and tribalism associated with an increase in education. But it is also true that there has been an increase in other social problems—crime and drugs, for example—associated with more education. In neither case are there clear, general causal associations. Education in itself will not make men into enlightened individuals. It would be a daring person who would argue that educational systems confer wisdom. An educational system is part of the society and culture in which it is embodied, and it cannot be separated from that society and culture. Although many burdens of solving social problems are put on educational systems, they cannot really do better than the societies which create and sustain them.

Suppose we can agree simply that education is a "good thing." Then more of it cannot hurt and is bound to do some good. When there is so much doubt about the details of investment allocation and social expenditure, can we make mistakes by putting more resources into education? The answer is yes. Devoting more resources to education means giving less to other developmental purposes where they might be more useful. And agreeing that education is a good thing does not help in deciding what kind of education to expand, what levels, and what types. One general proposition which has been advanced as a basis for allocation of funds is that the less-developed countries should concentrate their educational resources on the provision of vocational instruction. This proposition derives from the apparent unsuitability of conventional, Western, classical education to the context of developing countries. It has frequently been observed, with much scorn and hilarity, that it is incongruous to teach Latin, English and French history, etc., in Africa and Asia, for example. In many former English colonies there are high unemployment rates among college graduates with degrees in English literature while there is an obvious scarcity of persons with technical skills at professional and semi-professional and craftsmen levels.

Certainly there is a great deal to be criticized in the imposition of Western educational idiosyncracies on less-developed countries. It is not even clear that the conventional education is most appropriate in the United States and Western Europe. But we should also be aware that there have been many attempts to establish vocational education programs in less-developed countries, and many of these have not succeeded. There is a long history of failure, for example, in British Africa.

The failure of vocational education programs in less-developed countries has often had its source in the correct perception by individuals and families that there were greater opportunities for advancement through training which led into the government bureaucracy and clerical and management positions in private companies, paths of advancement which are reached through a standard education which emulates education of foreigners.

Thus the failure of government vocational education schemes has often represented failure to perceive that widespread general education is demanded and required in the course of development. It is also true, however, that such requirements are, in part, the result of the particular colonial pattern of development with limited economic change and slow growth, and, though it was often wrong in the past to attempt to impose vocational education on an agricultural society beyond the need for such education, it might be a mistake now to neglect vocational education in many countries where changes in economic structure are rapid.

A special rationale for the large-scale expansion of education has been that it provides a means of reducing inequalities in income and social status. This objective of education has been advanced for many years. It has an obvious appeal. Clearly, if only 10 percent of eligible children can find places in primary school, then there are fewer opportunities for reduction in inequality than if 100 percent of eligible children can find places in primary school. But does the argument hold for middle and higher education, in which there are never 100 percent of eligibles in school? There is a growing awareness that the educational systems in many less-developed countries have operated in a *regressive* manner. The lower income groups have, in effect, subsidized the education of upper and middle income groups. The result is a decrease in the equality of income and social status.

How has this result come about? First, access to middle and higher education in most less-developed countries is limited. Second, the children of middle and upper income classes are generally more successful in taking advantage of those opportunities which do exist than are the children of lower income groups. This is partly because at lower income levels there is greater pressure on young people to work in order to supplement the income of the family.

The family background at middle and upper income levels is more supportive and encouraging for students and provides more intellectual stimulation as well. In effect, the processes of advancement in the educational system result in middle and upper income groups' obtaining the largest benefits. That in itself is not surprising and would not make the system regressive if it were not for the fact that the educational system is supported by revenues from a tax system which is regressive. The tax systems of less-developed countries are dominated by indirect excise or sales taxes on major items of consumption. The excise taxes are a larger proportion of the income of lower income groups than for middle and upper income groups. While there are income taxes in less-developed countries which are usually progressive, these are not well enforced. So, in effect, there is relatively little reliance on such taxes.

The net effect is to make the relation between tax revenues and educational benefits regressive. Thus, instead of increasing equality, the tax and educational systems together tend to increase inequality—not an inevitable characteristic of educational systems in less-developed countries but one which is difficult to avoid, since it is difficult to change the tax system. It means, in turn, that special attention must be given to providing greater equality of opportunity within the educational system.

So much for the inadequacies of the conventional wisdom about education and development. Where is the truth?

How Can Decisions Be Made?

Consider for a moment the many issues which must be resolved in answering questions of educational policy. There must be decisions on such great questions as: How much primary education? How much secondary, and university-level, and professional education? And there must be a host of detailed decisions. How much medical education should there be? How much engineering? How much mathematics should be taught? How much economics?

In spite of a multitude of commissions which have met in many of the less-developed countries and in international agencies, the answers which have been given to these questions are seldom explicit. But it will help to review the methods which have already been used in trying to plan education and to consider whether they are, in principle, capable of giving answers to the questions which have been posed.

Three alternative approaches to educational policy making have been used. The first might be called "follow-the (or a)-leader." That is, pattern educational policy after the way it has been formulated in some apparently successfully developed country, i.e., the United States, the United Kingdom, France, Germany, the Netherlands, the Soviet Union, etc.

The second method of making overall educational policy is manpower planning. This procedure starts with forecasting needs for specific types of educated manpower required to operate a growing economy. Then, on the basis of projections of specific numbers of workers with particular types of training, it is possible to create an educational system to achieve these manpower goals at the times needed.

The third method is to calculate the return on inputs into education, treating education as if it were an investment. The rule then is to carry on the "investment in education" as long as its rate of return compares favorably with the rate on other types of investment.

A brief examination of these three alternative decision methods and their strengths and weaknesses will help reveal more about problems of educational decision making.

The follow-a-leader approach

The follow-a-leader approach implies the establishment in a less-developed country of a replica, with slight changes perhaps, of the educational system in some advanced country. The rationale is a simple one: It works in the advanced country; therefore, it must be an effective system and can work in the less-developed country as well. Often this rationale is overlaid or founded on cultural chauvinism. The patterns of education in the advanced country are thought by many persons, the foreign expert and the foreign-educated elite, to be obviously the superior way to do it, products of a superior culture, which should be made available to enlighten the poor ignorant brothers. The most obvious examples of this are the educational systems created by the French in their colonies. These systems were clearly meant to be extensions of the educational system of the mother state: to copy and to feed graduates into the educational system of France. The French language in particular was regarded as a superior instrument of culture and science and other languages obviously inferior—not just the dialects of Africa, but English and other languages as well.

Other examples of follow-a-leader are some of the missionary schools founded by religious groups in the less-developed areas. Although in many cases there was a sincere attempt in these schools to develop a pattern of education especially suited to the area in which the school was established, in many other cases the schools were formed to a pattern created in the advanced country from which the missionaries were sent. This was done in part to prepare students who would be able to follow the curriculum in the advanced school of the missionary group in the *metropole*.

But it would be a mistake to think that all the cases of follow-a-leader in educational policy were the result of imposition of educational patterns from outside. There are a variety of forces which impelled indigenous educational policy makers to believe that the best and correct education was the type offered in the more-developed countries. These leaders themselves usually had received their advanced education in the more-developed countries. They expected that the next generation or two of students would follow their own pattern.

In addition, it is a bold and risky undertaking to try to develop a country by laying out new and untried types of educational patterns. There is a lot to be said for reducing the risk of mistakes when the cost of mistakes is high, and in a less-developed country the cost of creating an educational system which does not work effectively is particularly high.

Suppose one took the follow-a-leader rationale seriously and attempted to apply it. Unless one were French the next question would be, What example should be followed? There are a number of different examples, and even a superficial survey of educational systems in the advanced countries indicates that they differ considerably.

As evidence of such differences, compare, from country to country, the so-called educational pyramids—pictures formed by graphs of the percentages of eligible persons in each age group in the country who are actually in school. The percentages are always higher for lower levels of education and lower for higher levels of education. Therefore the graph, with males on one side and females on the other, forms a pyramid. But educational pyramids differ greatly among the advanced countries. The U.S. educational pyramid has a broad base and tapers relatively gradually toward the point of high levels of professional and post-graduate education. The educational pyramids of most Western European countries, where relatively small proportions of persons participate in higher education and professional education, have a broad base but taper very sharply toward a spire.

Is it possible to say with any scientific conviction that one educational system has been more successful than another in development and growth terms? Not really, not at this time. Comparative studies of the economic and social effects of different educational systems are still in their infancy. Right now researchers are still at an early stage in the attempt to identify the essential differences between educational systems. It is a difficult job to untangle their distinctive effects from other sources of differences between countries. Still, while there should be a good deal of skepticism about blindly following the leader of one country or another in setting up educational systems, it is also necessary to recognize that there are good arguments for making educational policy by emulating at least selectively what has worked someplace else. At the outset of this discussion I argued that we really have relatively little understanding of how educational systems operate and also that we know little about the relation of educational systems to economic development. In such circumstances there is a good deal to be said for following a pattern which seems to have worked reasonably well in circumstances which are not too different. In fact, there is so much appeal to this approach that I shall return to it again and again.

The manpower-planning approach

Let me now turn to the manpower-planning approach to making educational policy. It has been advanced and has been used in a number of areas. Its logic has a powerful appeal because of its simple and straightforward nature. First of all, it rejects the policy of following the leader, or selective emulation, on the grounds that the economic structure of countries differs and, therefore, the outputs of the educational systems should also differ. Some countries are, and for a long time to come will continue to be, primarily agricultural in nature. Therefore, a relatively large proportion of their citizens should be trained for a farm life. Other countries will develop particular types of industry and should have more trained engineers and industrial workers. Some countries have a substantial cadre of primary- and intermediate-level school teachers and do not require emphasis on teacher training, but other countries do not have such a cadre and do need more teachers' colleges. In many countries the medical system is rudimentary and it is desirable to plan for more doctors, nurses, and medical technicians.

In the simple logic of the manpower-planning approach the occupational targets for the country must first be established. These must be based on output targets for the country's development. The output targets are transformed into employment goals on the basis of some projected ratios of output to labor input. The overall employment goals are then broken down into occupational employment targets, again using some standard ratios of types of employment to total employment.

For example, the output of the engineering industry may be projected for 1975, 1980, 1985, and so on into the future. From this the employment in the industry is projected on the basis of an estimated ratio of so many workers per dollar or rupee of engineering goods output. Then it might be estimated that, say, one in ten workers must be a professional engineer, two workers in ten must be skilled craftsmen, five in ten must be semi-skilled operatives, and the remainder will be unskilled workers. In this way we project a total engineering labor force for the engineering goods industry with the total, in turn, refined into separate numbers of mechanical engineers, electrical engineers, industrial engineers, craftsmen, operatives, and so on. This is done for each sector of the economy so we finally have a total number of, say, mechanical engineers needed in the economy in 1975, 1980, 1985, and so on. We know how many mechanical engineers there are in 1973, so we can figure out how many more must be trained in the future.

With such detailed manpower totals it is then possible to compute how many students must be admitted to engineering schools, to medical schools, to teachers' colleges, and so on. Working back still further, it is possible to compute how many students must be admitted to high school to get enough students out of high school with the necessary levels of achievement to be successful in the professional schools, given the expected rate of attrition there. Thus, output and targets can be projected back through the educational system. The manpower-planning approach requires some specification of teaching methods, of course, because it is necessary to take account of the manpower requirements for the educational system as well. But that planning is also done on the basis of ratios which are calculated from past patterns.

Manpower planning has been applied in many countries, including the United States. Perhaps its most obvious application is in the military services, which project their manpower requirements by particular occupations and develop their training programs to meet these requirements. But private companies also make such projections and plan training programs in much the same way.

In the 1960s a number of the less-developed European countries around the Mediterranean also adopted a manpower-planning approach. With the help of the Organization for Economic Cooperation and Development, a Meditterranean Manpower Planning Project was established, in which a common set of manpower-planning techniques was prepared and followed to form a basis for educational policy in the countries. This Mediterranean Project provides some experience which permits us to judge the techniques.

Unfortunately, an examination of that experience does not permit a great deal of confidence in the manpower-planning method. The reason is clear. Everything hangs on those critical ratios of total employment to total output and of employment in particular occupations to total employment. Just small changes in those ratios are enough to throw the results off a good deal. And in the course of development, as the productivity of labor changes with changes in technology, the ratios *are* likely to change.

There are other deep social and economic reasons for the change in the ratios and for changes in the character of occupations as well. The work arrangements and manpower-staffing patterns of each country reflect the social structure of each country and not just technology and economics. Each society will change in the course of development, that we know. But we cannot predict exactly how it will change. Occupational definitions change in the course of development as well. For example, government clerks who were once regarded as superior beings in many countries may become ordinary mortals. And the educational background for such clerks may change as a consequence.

In addition, there is usually more than one way to fill the manpower requirements for any level and type of output. For example, every country in the course of development will demand improvements in its medical system. That means more doctors will be necessary. If a doctor were a standard commodity it would be possible to predict how many doctors would be required for future improvements in medical care. But doctors are not standard commodities. They vary from country to country as well as within countries in the content and quality of their training. We have the impression, for example, that doctors in the Soviet Union are, on the average, less intensively trained than U.S. doctors. That is not to say that they are not as well trained, because they may be trained quite well enough for what the average doctor in the USSR is called upon to do. However, medical training in the USSR seems to be combined differently than it is in this country. And the medical care provided for most citizens of the Soviet Union may well be just as good as that provided most citizens in the United States.

On closer examination, therefore, the simple logic of manpower planning seems too simple to be a reliable method of making educational policy. While it may provide some guidelines, it should not guide all of educational policy.

The rate-of-return approach

The final method of educational decision making to be described is also one which has a good deal of appeal. And it too has a simple and powerful logic that appears to overcome many problems. Just think of education as if it were an investment. There are many similarities between getting an education and investing in a factory or an electrical generating station. Both take a considerable amount of time, using up resources all the while in the process. And both have long-lasting effects in increased output capability. The way to decide whether to invest in a factory or in an electricity-generating station is to figure out how it will pay off, that is, compute the rate of return on the investment. Well then, just do the same for education.

To compute the rate of return on, say, a college education or a mechanical engineering education, or a doctor's education, first one must measure all the costs. These will include the direct costs of teachers' salaries and of books and other equipment. Another, indirect cost will be what economists call the "opportunity cost" to the student himself. If he were not spending his time in school for his education, he could be at work earning some income. Part of the cost of keeping the student in school, therefore, is the income which he sacrifices by not holding the job he could otherwise have had. If he would not have been able to obtain a job, that cost is zero. But usually people of student calibre are employable, at first maybe only for part-time work, but then, with more experience, full time. So the opportunity costs of income sacrificed by the student's being in school become quite considerable, particularly at higher levels.

Now imagine all the costs, direct and indirect, being added up to obtain the total cost of each year of education.

The next step is more difficult. It is to compute the extra income earned by the student which can be attributed to his extra education—and *only* to his extra education. That is usually done by comparing the incomes of persons of the same age but with different levels of education. The differences in income are then attributed to differences in education.

There is quite a large professional literature which reflects continuing debate over the reliability of this way of identifying the income-earning effects of education. It is easy to think of a number of influences other than education which would create differences between the incomes of persons who also have different educational backgrounds. Individual intelligence, family social status, family professional status, and differences in intellectual quality of home life all contribute to income differences. They also make education more or less effective than it would otherwise have been.

There are still other problems involved in identifying the effects of education, however. There is the problem of forecasting over an individual's lifetime the effect of more or less education at an early age. There is the problem that the rates of payment which individuals receive—and which are related to educational differences—may not reflect the productivity of the individuals and their education, because the labor markets which determine payment rates may not, for a variety of reasons, be competitive. So the pricing of different types of labor and total labor incomes may be misleading with respect to the true economic contribution of education.

An example may help clarify the problems which arise in using the rate-of-return approach. One of the few applications of the method was in suggesting educational policy in Nigeria. I examined that analysis on the basis of my own research. I had formed the hypothesis that some of the highest returns to education among the various occupations were in government bureaucracies. Some calculations I had done, for the United States particularly, indicated this. In the less-developed countries, where the bureaucracies are even more powerful than they are here, I expected that bureaucrats would also be more successful than they are here in applying political pressure to obtain high salaries for themselves. While I do not wish to denigrate the contribution of government bureaucracies to development, it would be a rash man who claimed that the incomes of bureaucrats reflect their economic contributions rather than their political power.

One must also recognize that a relatively large proportion of high school and college trained people in Nigeria work in the government. So the political power of the Nigerian bureaucracy has a particularly heavy weight in determining the average incomes of persons with these levels of education. The results, which called for much more high school and college education, took that form in large part because education seemed to be doing so much good for government bureaucrats. But that certainly does not mean it is doing as much good for the economy as a whole. The rate-of-return calculation was misleading, because the assumptions on which it was based were not correct.

To summarize, all of the methods for making educational policy which have been used have grave deficiencies. These arise partly because of a lack of information, and more fundamentally, because the nature of the relation of education to economic development is not well understood. It is a complex and subtle relation, while the approaches which have been followed are simple and mechanical. In such circumstances what constructive suggestions can be made about how much and what kind of education should be provided for economic development? This review has exposed the weakness of the various approaches to educational policy making. It is necessary to rethink the problem without reliance on old devices or methodologies.

Suggestions for Educational Guidelines for Development

It is not possible, I believe, to prescribe a general educational policy for every less-developed country. There are few, if any, general rules, and every country requires its own study. Some minimum guidelines for educational programs can be suggested, however.

What is required for educational equity?

In order to formulate an equitable educational program it is, first of all, necessary to decide on the meaning of educational equity. A number of alternative meanings will be surveyed briefly here and their relative costs and feasibility roughly assessed.

The most ambitious of equity goals is equality of educational achievement for everyone of equal talent. This is ambitious, because in no society will the "extracurricular" social system prepare persons of equal talent so that they can all benefit equally from the schooling system. So this educational equity goal requires that the schooling system *compensate* for any inequalities created outside the system. Moreover, this goal requires that the schooling system persist until persons of equal talent reach equal achievement. Given its ambitious character, this goal may be attainable only if there is relatively limited educational achievement for everyone. Persons of higher talent may have to be neglected in order to devote more resources to persons of lower talent for the sake of achieving equality. For example, there is little doubt that most eligible children can successfully complete a high school level education. Yet, if a high school level of learning were guaranteed to any and every child in many of the less-developed countries, a many-fold expansion of the educational system would be required. It would mean drastic increases in the educational budget. Goals less ambitious than this were established for some African countries after their independence, perhaps for different reasons, and it became clear after some time that they simply were not achievable with the resources available to the country.

The costs to society include more than the direct educational costs, however. If egalitarianism means that the most talented members of any generation do not receive an education which brings their full talents to fruition, all of society is likely to suffer in economic and cultural terms. So the benefits of such egalitarianism must be weighed against substantial costs.

Equality of *schooling* for everyone of equal talent is a less radical proposal than the attempt to equalize *learning*. Equality of schooling only requires that equals be treated equally in the number of years they spend in schools, not that the attempt be made to insure that the same amount of learning be achieved. It is, in fact, much closer to the policies actually followed when the stated goal is equality of treatment for persons of equal talent.

This goal of equal schooling is also expensive in relation to the resources which are available, however. We know this, because it is this goal which countries like Nigeria and Ghana actually tried to achieve and found beyond their reach. It is not beyond the reach of the more advanced countries, though there are few, if any, which do achieve it. It is within reach for the United States and for the Western European countries. Compared with other nations, the United States has come closest to achieving the goal; Western Europe is probably far behind.

Not only is the goal of equal schooling for equal talents likely to be beyond the reach of the less-developed countries, it may be socially unwise as well, at least in one sense. Achievement of the goal would create many more relatively highly educated persons than many economies can absorb at the levels to which they would aspire. The phenomenon of educated unemployed is increasingly familiar in the less-developed countries of the world. The educated unemployed have aspirations which their country cannot fulfill. They are not as mobile downwards as they are upwards. They do not fill up the occupations of clerks and sales-persons, of factory workers and farmers and craftsmen. These occupations are left to the relatively uneducated, and the more educated unemployed remain unemployed for long periods of time. Anyone advocating the goal of equal schooling for equal talents must seriously consider whether it is worth the frustration and unhappiness associated with aspirations which are likely to remain unsatisfied for long periods of time.

It is claimed that the educated unemployed are a major source of social unrest in urban areas. They are supposed to be the ones who riot in the street and overthrow governments—only to find that the next government is no more successful in solving their unemployment problems than the previous one. Meanwhile the disorder which they create is a major barrier to successful economic growth. But, while there may be something in this argument, we actually know relatively little about the sources of political and social unrest in less-developed countries.

The goal of equality of *opportunity* for schooling and education for persons of equal talent is possible to achieve without incurring unbearable economic burdens, depending of course on how such equality of opportunity is defined. Let me propose a minimum definition: persons of equal talent have the same chance to acquire equal schooling.

An example will help to illustrate the minimal ways in which this equity goal can be defined. Suppose that it were somehow decided that only 10 percent of the persons capable of benefiting from a college education could benefit the economy and could be absorbed in the educational system. Then we would have to find some method for choosing one in ten from the eligible group which would give every eligible an equal chance. One method would be to draw lots so that the choice is made by chance. That is never done. Charging a high tuition is another rationing device, one which benefits the children of the upper income groups particularly. That is a device which has been used over and over again. Locating the schools of higher education in urban areas, with no help to rural children for support in these areas, is another method of rationing which does not provide equal opportunity.

Whatever the manner in which equity is defined, a major problem for equity goals is that of identifying persons of equal talent. Because of the way social systems work, some persons can be easily overlooked. There are no tests which will, with a high degree of reliability, identify different degrees of native talent. One of the few lessons which we have learned about education is that the schooling process itself not only provides education, it is a method of selecting persons who will benefit from more education.

Therefore, even the limited equity goal of equality of opportunity for persons of equal talent may require a substantial amount of education just to establish the composition of the talent pools. It might even be argued that equality of opportunity requires compensatory education programs. That in effect is part of the logic for the various "Head Start" programs in the United States, which try to compensate with schooling techniques for relatively disadvantaged social backgrounds so that children will have equal opportunity to benefit from regular schools. Equality of opportunity for persons of equal talent would appear to require, at the least, a comprehensive program in the primary grades of schooling. As long as tests are inadequate, some amount of schooling for everyone is necessary just to determine who has talent and is eligible to be chosen for more schooling.

However, I do not think that equity considerations will take us much further in designing education for less-developed areas. I shall turn next to output criteria to determine how far they will take us.

What Amounts of Education Are Required?

Finally, it is necessary to come to a decision about the method to be used for projecting economic requirements for education. The one which I propose is a variation of manpower planning with careful examination of economic conditions in order to insure consistency between manpower plans and occupational compensation.

First of all it is necessary to recognize that only a limited number of occupations require long-range planning. A study which I did a number of years ago of the U.S. labor force in 1950 indicated that less than 8 percent of the labor force at that time required a general college education in order to be able to turn in an average level of performance. And only 4 percent of the labor force required more than four years of specific vocational preparation. These numbers for the U.S. labor force are not directly applicable for manpower planning in less-developed countries for a number of reasons. First of all there are many qualifications and sources of possible error in my study. Secondly, even if the numbers are correct, they may not represent an optimal adjustment but one which may be more or less than desirable. Thirdly, there is probably important interaction between the amount of general education which exists in the population and the amount of specific vocational preparation which is required in the labor force. In particular, general education may to some extent be a substitute for vocational preparation. Thus, a reduction in general education may require a compensating increase in vocational education in order to maintain labor efficiency.

Nonetheless, I believe that there is a lesson of general applicability which can be drawn from this early study: It is not necessary to do detailed manpower planning for the entire labor force far in advance of actual needs. That kind of planning need be done only for a small proportion of occupations and persons. These will be primarily in the professions, of course. And, in turn, the planning there is relatively straightforward, although important options for flexibility should also be recognized.

The flexibility arises because some substitution of less for more highly educated persons is possible in nearly all professions. Doctors can serve as nurses and nurses can replace doctors in many kinds of activities, and to an increasing extent that is being done. For example, a new occupation of so-called paramedical technicians is developing in the United States to replace M.D.'s with four years of medical school with persons who have two years of specialized training beyond college. Likewise a new occupation of paralegal assistants is developing to replace full-fledged lawyers in some activities with persons with less training. Although I have never heard of paraengineers, it is well known that foremen and technicians can replace college-trained engineers in many kinds of activities, and that is done as a matter of course.

Before long-range manpower planning is undertaken for those few occupations in which it is necessary, a careful cost-benefit study of the alternative ways of performing the functions carried out by persons in those occupations is desirable. The study may indicate it is unnecessary to follow previously established patterns and that there are important cost savings which can be achieved by the substitution of lower-level manpower for higher-level manpower.

In any case, some kind of long-range manpower planning will have to be done. Projections will have to be made of so many new doctors, so many new engineers, etc., which will have to be turned out by the educational system each year in the future. Those forecasts will in turn lead to designs for the educational system itself—so many new engineering schools, so many teachers of engineering, and so on.

I would make only one other recommendation for less-developed countries with respect to manpower which requires long periods of time for training: avoid fads and fashions—in particular, and maybe especially, those in science. Science education is among the most expensive types in its direct costs and in the length of time it requires. Most of the less-developed countries do not require much scientific personnel for their economic development. Scientists and schools of science are like pyramids and national monuments—expensive and nonproductive symbols. Other symbols are available which cost less than a Nobel prize biochemist. Choose the other symbols. And exploit the scientific establishment in the more-advanced countries both for education of those scientists which are required in the less-developed countries and also for the direct scientific inputs which are required.

Both equity and narrow economic considerations suggest that there be a broad base of general education. That broad base will help fill the specific occupational requirements which will emerge in the course of development. Children who have been taught to read and write and to do elementary arithmetic will be able to learn to operate machine tools faster than they otherwise would; and they will also have an opportunity that they otherwise would not have had to be chosen for higher education.

It was fashionable some time ago to praise a general liberal arts education essentially on vocational grounds—that it is the best type of "training for life," on the presumption that life is going to present many challenges which cannot be accurately foreseen. There is a great deal to be said for that argument. Yet for a developing country the challenges of life can be foreseen to some degree. In that case, they can be planned for with some type of manpower planning, remembering always not to be too rigid. But for many of the exigencies which cannot be foreseen, the best motto is "stay loose." Don't make too specific a commitment. Provide the kind of general education which prepares for a variety of careers.

Notice that I have specifically not recommended rate-of-return calculations. Those estimates embody so many conditions which are bound to change and so much market imperfection that I believe they are useless in making future policy. Simple manpower plans are simple-minded but at least their assumptions and their consequences are clear.

I believe that educational policy in less-developed countries is *not* a field in which the important next step is the development of sophisticated planning models. I have worked on a variety of such planning models in other aspects of development for less-developed countries when I thought that the essential simplifications which are involved did not do so much violence to reality as to make the models unusable. Furthermore, in the case of overall economic development, the essential goals can be formulated in a relatively straightforward manner. But I think the field of education does not meet these conditions for sophisticated modeling.

Education displays complex interaction with social change as well as its simpler economic function of providing skilled manpower. The considerable flexibility in staffing patterns and the potential mobility of workers among jobs also complicate educational planning. A machine tool is a machine tool and that for all of its life. But a construction worker need not be a construction worker all of *his* life. He may have started as a farmer and may end as a factory worker, having been at some other time a taxi driver or stevedore. The characteristic simplifications of planning models in other areas seem to be particularly inappropriate in the field of education.

Thus there are no grand and simple methods and no great simplifying insights which will provide guides to educational policy. Educational policy is and will remain one of the most difficult kinds of social policy to formulate.

Perhaps the most important thing to be said about making such policy is that inflexible programs which involve major commitments in great detail should be avoided. They are almost certain to lead to major mistakes. One should try hard to create opportunities both for individuals and for the economy as a whole to be flexible. When knowledge is gravely limited, as it is in this field, great mistakes can be made by holding to the view that knowledge is certain.

INVESTMENTS IN OURSELVES: OPPORTUNITIES AND IMPLICATIONS

THEODORE W. SCHULTZ

As members of a college audience, you are proud of your idealism and critical of the mundane realism that characterizes economic affairs. In your perspective people who are pure capitalists are beyond the pale of a good society. At the risk of alienating you I shall argue that you are shrewd, calculating capitalists. You are capitalists striving to add to your private stock of human capital, an important form of capital which is increasing in proportion to the stock of material capital (property assets) in our society. Furthermore, in your capitalistic behavior your social concern is on a par with those capitalists' whom you so readily criticize. Neither they nor you are conspicuously benevolent.

In becoming a capitalist, you are making sacrifices. You are using your own time and the resources of your family and of society for the process of investing in yourself to enhance your future private satisfactions and earnings. Fortunately, there are more opportunities to invest in yourself in our society than in most other societies. There are also more opportunities to do so at present than in any preceding generation.

This process of adding to the stock of your human capital began in the family context, when you were an infant, and it was strongly linked to the time and attention that your mother devoted then to enhancing your abilities. Elementary and high school followed, and as you advanced additional options were available to you, consisting of more formal education and of on-the-job training following high school or college. Then, too, throughout your lifetime you can invest in your health and in improving your economic lot by means of geographical migration, and in your effectiveness as a consumer and producer by searching for and using information.

In economic analysis four important recent developments pertain to these investments we make in ourselves. The concept of human capital is one of them. Out of this concept, specifically out of the earnings-foregone notion, came the theory of the allocation of human time, developed by Gary Becker in his seminal paper in the *Economic Journal* of September 1965. The recent extension and adaptation of the production function to the household—seeing the household as a producing unit—brought the activities of the household into the domain of economic analysis. These extensions of theory have made possible the new economic approaches to productiveness presented in the March/April 1973 *Supplement* to the *Journal of Political Economy*. Seeing the value of the time of females and analyzing household activities using a household production function reveal new economic insights. Then too there is the extension in theory, first presented by George Stigler, on the cost and returns associated with the search for information.

My presentation, which will be restricted to the educational sector of the United States, will consist mainly of an overview of higher education. I shall begin with four propositions pertaining to higher education on which a part of the analysis that follows rests. I shall then criticize several major unwarranted expectations that are widely held with regard to higher education. Thirdly, I shall review the current economic prospects for higher education, and lastly I shall consider several important implications of my approach.

Four Basic Propositions

The following propositions are basically valid. I present them with very little supporting argument.

1. *The social benefits of a college education are very much overrated.* Our talk stressing such social benefits represents a self-serving view that we in highereducation find ever so comfortable. We like to have people believe that our college education benefits those who pay a part of the bill, among whom there are many who have or will have received less education than we have. According to this view, there are important social benefits, in addition to the benefits that accrue to you and to your classmates. We have invented a long list of such social benefits which are supported, not by evidence, but by rhetoric. For example, it is said over and over again that a person with a bachelor's degree is, because of his education, a better citizen that the less-educated person. But where is the evidence that this is true? I know of none that shows that people with four years of college have

better citizenship records because of their education than do people with a high-school education. Let me leave this issue at that.
2. *College students are in general efficient in allocating their time and funds in acquiring a college education.* There is considerable evidence to support this statement in Richard Freeman's book on college-educated people.[1] In addition, his recent evidence shows a rapid response to the new opportunities that have opened up since the middle sixties for black college-educated males in the United States. This is strong evidence of the economic calculus at work once opportunities are at hand. I would venture the view that college students are, in general, as efficient in this context as firms for profit are in their domain.
3. In the allocation of public funds to schooling and higher education in the United States, *too few sources are provided for the lower levels of schooling compared to those that go into higher education.* In an examination of the different levels of education, the economic evidence convinces me that an additional million dollars allocated to the lowest level would add more benefits than the same amount of additional expenditure would add on the highest level. This means that, at this juncture in our history, the highest priority should be assigned to assisting mothers who have had the least schooling so they can give their infant children a better start.
4. An important proposition pertains to on-campus research activities. *Where a faculty is competent to do research, research is basically an investment in public goods.* To the extent that society wants these public goods, such research must be financed by society. For example, the advances in science that led to hybrid corn, wheat, and other crops are an important factor in recent increases in crop yields; these advances from this research were published in national and international biological journals. They were not patented; they are public goods.

Four Unwarranted Expectations

Many of the much-discussed "defects" in our system of higher education are so categorized on the basis of inferences derived from unwarranted expectations.

It is frequently said that, while other sectors of the economy achieve large gains in the productivity of labor, it is evident that higher education has failed to stay abreast of industry and agriculture by this test. But the long-run decline in the manhours required to produce a bushel of wheat is

---

[1]. *The Market for College-Trained Manpower: A Study in the Economics of Career Choice* (Cambridge, Mass.: Harvard University Press, 1971).

simply not applicable as a test in determining the manhours of instruction that are necessary per college student. While there are undoubtedly some possibilities for economizing on the time of teachers, the expectation that there might be large gains in labor productivity in instruction if colleges could be made efficient is wholly unwarranted.

Another much-touted "defect" of education in general and of higher education in particular is the notion popularized by Jencks that education is not eliminating inequalities. Of course it is not. But the odd notion that it should, rests on the false belief that higher education is a welfare activity. The solution of the welfare-equity problem of society calls for generalized income and wealth adjustment; the instruction and research functions of higher education are not activities of which the objective is to solve the pervasive welfare-equity problems. Recent studies of higher education in California and Florida contain some evidence that this part of education is regressive in its effects on the personal distribution of income. Although the studies are subject to criticism, the basic issue that they bring to the fore is that of who should pay for this higher education and not whether higher education should be transformed into a welfare agency. Welfare is elusive. Consider the point that when disadvantaged students are subsidized the youth whose family is poor and who does not qualify is then discriminated against, because he is then left in a worse position relatively, in the sense that the gap between those who qualify and those who do not has been widened.

There is also the unwarranted expectation that increases of public funds do not result in more public control of higher education. But the fact is that public funds for higher education imply public control. The Carnegie Commission Report on higher education is strangely silent on this issue. It simply says that universities need billions of additional dollars of federal funds but never a word that this implies additional federal control. This issue can be put very simply: No government can divest itself of the responsibility of seeing to it that public funds are used for the purposes for which they are appropriated. This responsibility implies public control.

Last on my list of unwarranted expectations is the belief that the politics of providing public funds for higher education concern the *quality* of the instruction as much as the *quantity* of instruction. I would not hesitate to predict that our legislative bodies will continue for years to come to insist on quantity, not quality.

Economic Effects of the Boom Years

I now turn to the adverse economic developments affecting higher education that have occurred since the late sixties. Is higher education in for a long depressed period? The view of faculty and administrators is one of pessimism. This view is clearly expressed in a recent report to the now defunct Science Advisory Committee to the President. It points out that many college graduates become teachers and there is an oversupply of teachers. It also argues that for demographic reasons the supply of young people who will want to enter the labor market is going to be larger than normal and that even more of these young people than would otherwise will opt for college. It is obvious that the demand for teachers is down sharply and that the demographic flood of young people during the coming decade is a fact. Furthermore, the report argues that the demand for high skills (Ph.D.'s) is being reduced by the reductions in R and D funds provided by the federal government.

What is missing in the report to the Science Advisory Committee is notice of the fairly rapid adjustments that college students are making to the changes in job opportunities for college graduates. The implication of these adjustments is that the depressed earnings of recent graduates will be of short duration. I venture the prediction that even the demand for chemists within five years will show that the drop in the number of chemistry Ph.D.'s during the last several years will turn out to have been an overadjustment. Presently, prospective graduate students are avoiding this field with the consequence that a shortage is in the making.

For our campuses, however, the adjustments are more difficult. Colleges and universities must adjust to the fact that they operated in a boom period from the mid-fifties to close to the end of the sixties. This boom created distortions within the educational system, but the distortions are not evidence that there is going to be a much smaller demand for college-educated people. In discussing these distortions I will probably step on some sensitive toes.

During the recent boom in college funds, we spent too much on campus buildings and on expensive equipment, and thus we are now overextended on such physical capital. It is largely sunk investment, and some of it appears quite serious. Salvaging it is beset with difficulties. For example, consider the University of Southern Illinois at Carbondale: an array of new beautiful buildings, marvelous settings, and all manner of equipment. Even in coping with the hot summer, there are excellent air conditioning facilities to accommodate a large national professional conference. An overcommitment to structures and equipment is one aspect of the institutional adjustment problem.

Another aspect is the fact that promotions came too fast and too easily, and many campuses are now stuck with too many faculty who were granted tenure too soon. In most departments—biology, mathematics, economics, or what have you—given the market demand for instructors (professors) created by the rapid expansion that was going on in most of the 1960s, tenure was part of the necessary price. (Also, it might be noted, during the boom years not a few members of the faculty bargained themselves out of teaching to the point that they impaired their on-campus instruction.) Now these departments find themselves with too many tenured faculty members. In retrospect, some of these promotions, a response to the market price at the time they were made, can be seen as a mistake. Clearly this distortion is going to create a lot of heartaches for the new crop of instructors who can't get promoted. How does a university correct that kind of maladjustment?

Along with the rapid promotions, salaries are somewhat inflated, and so are fringe benefits. Oblivious to the market, we now espouse the fiction that we, the faculty, know that our salaries are too low. A faculty may act as a monopoly but not for long. Changes in supply and demand really matter. During the fifties and sixties I also profited. It was a time when the academic market favored me in selling my services, and the poor buyer, the university, had to pay dearly. Presently, our salaries are somewhat too high competitively in the American scene. If salaries over the next few years were to rise at no more than half of the rate of inflation, they would probably be about in line. It is, of course, not in your private interest to accept this adjustment.

It is hard to find out how colleges are correcting the distortions caused by the recent boom and at what rate they are doing it. Is there a marked difference in the adjustment lags among different classes of colleges? My guess is that, in general, private colleges have been compelled to make adjustments sooner than public colleges. From a sample of one, I know that the hard realities of the budget at the University of Chicago began to call for adjustments at least three years ago. Tuitions have been increased each year. The size of the faculty has been reduced, and there have been no across-the-board increases in salaries. More important is the process of reexamining the many activities of the University and reordering the priorities in line with what is deemed to be the comparative advantage of the University. Some programs we started during the boom have turned out not to be essential to the core of the University of Chicago; these programs are being phased out. We are actually going to come out of this period of adjustment stronger rather than weaker. We are continuing to reallocate our funds gradually, painfully, shifting them to where they really belong. I venture that major adjustments of this type have occurred to a lesser extent at public universities. Private universities are much deeper into this adjustment process, not because they are more virtuous, but for reasons of plain necessity.

Conclusion

In closing, I shall review briefly and somewhat extend several of the implications of the preceding analysis.

Among the many behavioral attributes of college students, the one that I have featured is that students are increasing their private stock of human capital. In making this investment in themselves, college students are shrewd, calculating capitalists. I have argued that college students are, in general, efficient in allocating their own time and funds in acquiring a college education. A major implication of this proposition is that public and private subsidies to pay for college instruction should go to the students directly, not indirectly via subsidies to colleges and universities. The economic objective of this procedure is not to win the political support of students but to strengthen the forces of competition by compelling colleges and universities to become efficient, to provide instruction that would be good enough and cheap enough so that students, buyers of their services, would come to them.

The key implication of the proposition that the social benefits of higher education are much overrated is that most of the benefits accrue as private benefits to students. It follows that students (their families) should pay for these private benefits. In view of the high levels of personal income of most families in the United States, most college students should be paying the *full cost* of the instruction they receive. Economists are rightly appalled by the vast public subsidies which are paid to the shipping interests, to the fuel (oil) sector, and the farmers with the largest incomes. That our rich college students enrolled in private colleges pay only about 45 percent of the full costs of instruction they receive and those enrolled in public college very much less—i.e., about 15 percent—is also appalling.

In the allocation of public funds at this juncture in our history, elementary schools in financially poor districts and programs to assist mothers who have the least schooling so that they can do better by their infant children should be given a higher priority than college instruction. Then, too, the economics of university research indicate that public and private funds made available for this purpose should meet the test of increasing the supply of public goods. In the United States the social rates of return from these activities appear, in general, to be relatively high.

Competent criticism of higher education is a rare commodity, whereas pronouncements on what is wrong are abundant and cheap. Only a few years ago it was fashionable on the part of many college students to demand "relevance," the politicalization of universities, and a large measure of control in making appointments and promotions. Now it is fashionable to contend that there should be large gains in the labor productivity of college teachers, that colleges are discriminating against minorities and women, that colleges should engage much more than they do in welfare activities, that colleges are not reducing inequalities, and now, to top it off, we have Jencks's contention that education does not matter.

It does not call for much economic sophistication to know that some economic activities consist mainly of highly labor-intensive personal services. In these activities gains in labor productivity are, as a rule, hard to come by. Teaching has the attributes of such an activity, but this characterization does not imply that there are no serious inefficiencies imbedded in routine college instruction.

It requires more economic sophistication to see that the core of the welfare-equity problem of our society is beyond the domain of the basic functions of colleges and universities. Even subsidizing disadvantaged college students, while it reduces one type of inequality, introduces a new form of discrimination by widening the gap between those who qualify and those who do not (or do not opt for college).

Quality of instruction does matter, and many students or their families, want to buy this quality. But the federal government and most state governments are quantity oriented. The burden of counteracting this political pressure for quantity must be borne by the faculty and the administrations of public colleges and universities. Moreover, federal agencies in allocating federal funds to institutions of higher education are now seeking to control some important aspects of the management of higher education by establishing faculty quotas in the appointment and promotion of minority numbers and women. Personnel policy is only one of many areas in which additional federal funds lead to additional federal controls. Social scientists and economists, who are especially vulnerable to restrictions on criticism of social and economic policies, should be in the vanguard in revealing these dangers and eliminating them whenever they become evident.

I hope that I have not alienated the students and faculty in my audience by treating students as realistic, efficient capitalists in adding to their private human capital; by arguing that most students should pay the full cost of their education; and by featuring the overall adverse effects of the faculty's pursuit of self-interest in its opposition to the adjustments which recent changes in the market for academic personnel require.

METHODS OF FINANCE AND THE ORGANIZATION AND ADMINISTRATION OF LOCAL SCHOOLS

JERRY MINER

Introduction

I am going to discuss the financing of local schools. However, in many ways my remarks will not take the usual form in which economists, especially public finance economists, talk about school finance. It is my belief that the essential problems of local schools in the United States derive from the overall system of school governance and control and not primarily from finances. Therefore, reform of the way in which local schools are financed, no matter how extensive, will not come to grips with the most important issues involved in the provision of services by local schools. Consequently I will discuss school finance in the context of the general governance of local schools. This subject will inevitably take me into questions of governance and administration by local governments and into problems of service delivery by local government. To focus on the role of finance and to provide a perspective for examining and evaluating our American approach to the governance of local schools, I will emphasize comparisons of the ways in which schools are financed in certain of the economically and socially most advanced countries of Western Europe.

My objectives, then, are two-fold. First, to indicate the unusual and dominant role which finance plays in the system of governance of local schools in the United States. Second, to show that throughout the world a variety of combinations of financial, legislative, and administrative controls are used to influence the characteristics of schools and the services which they provide, and that observation of these alternative systems will teach us a good deal, if we wish to alter our system of local school government—as I believe we must.

Note: I would like to thank the Ford Foundation and the Higher Education Research Unit of the London School of Economics and Political Science whose support made possible the research on which this lecture is based.

School Finance and the Finance of Local Governments

Most discussions of school finance in the United States today concentrate on describing the existing inequalities in the distribution of tax bases among local school authorities and the resulting disparities in expenditures. Then, the discussions go on to propose alternative financing schemes which are intended to reduce or eliminate the relation of expenditures to the per capita income or to the per-pupil property valuation of the authority. Such analysis has been extremely useful in pointing up some extraordinary, indeed disgraceful, fiscal inequities. But, if we have learned anything from the past decade's worth of studies of educational performance and achievement, it is that there is no simple relationship between spending and learning.

Now, let me quickly make clear that I am not arguing here, as some have argued on the basis of these findings, that, because increased school spending is not lways associated with higher student performances on various achievement tests, disparities in spending, which seem always to favor wealthy areas, should be ignored or accepted. Unquestionably it is extremely important and worthwhile to reduce widespread differences between communities in the tax effort required to provide given revenues for schools and for other services as well.

What I do wish to argue is that a reform of school finance which simply equalizes expenditures or tax effort per dollar of expenditures will not meet the primary problems of local schools. These difficulties do not lie in local schools' lack of resources or even in the inequitable burdens of their finance. Rather these problems concern how to provide services that meet the needs of both the students and of the society at large. They are questions of who determines the extent to which schools are differentiated by purpose, climate, style, and instructional methods and who establishes the social, cultural, economic, and intellectual bases for assigning pupils to particular schools and tracks within schools. Finance may and usually does influence these matters, but the relation of finance to these substantive characteristics of schools differs under alternative systems of school governance. To look only at finance conceals the real questions of educational reform. Thus, proposals for reform of school finance must be viewed in light of the entire system of school governance. Here, because our own state school systems are politically and administratively similar, international comparisons can provide important insights regarding the operation of alternative systems.

Perhaps a few words of clarification will be useful at this point. There is no doubt that the central cities and certain suburban authorities in the

United States face serious fiscal problems. A move toward increased centralization of public school finance, if it took proper account of the so-called municipal overburdened, could ease the fiscal difficulties of the cities and at the same time, if it adjusted for the low property values of certain areas, it could equalize the burden of providing minimum levels of schooling. Yet the fiscal effects on local governments of modifications in school finance are only marginally more important than would be the effects of changes in the financing of other local government services such as protection, sanitation, transportation, welfare, and health. That is, the fiscal problem of local government service delivery is a general one and is not confined to schools. The great concern over school finance, in one sense, simply reflects the dominance of local schools in the budgets of local governments, where they account for over 45 percent of spending.

There is, however, another perspective on the importance of the finance of local schools. This perspective is not in terms of the overall fiscal burden of schools but in terms of the relation of the details of the financing mechanism to the characteristics of the schools. In this sense school finance and its reform cannot be separated from the organization and administration of schools. Reform of school finance will, of course, inevitably modify aspects of administration and organization. However, instead of awaiting such changes, surely we wish to anticipate some of the effects of changing the financing of the system and to speculate on certain of the concomitant changes in aspects of organization and administration which may be necessary or desirable under alternative methods of finance. One of the few ways of obtaining insights into how alternative mechanisms of control of a social institution work is through international comparisons. Great as are the difficulties with them, such comparisons can be extremely revealing. I shall try to draw some insights about the relation of school finance and governance from international comparisons and leave to you the judgment of whether the difficulties exceed the accomplishments.

School Finance and the Governance of Schools

There is little doubt that the dominant issue regarding local school policy in the United States today is finance. The newspapers, national magazines, and even television, as well as professional educational publications and journals are all discussing various crises in school finance. Among the issues raised are the funding difficulties in central cities, such as Detroit, the implications of the federal and state court cases challenging the use of local government revenues to support public schools, the so-called circuit-breaker proposal for property tax relief for the elderly, and President Nixon's attempt to compress some thirty conditional federal grants-in-aid to local schools into five categories of special revenue sharing. There is good reason for this predominance of concern about finance when educational policies and issues are raised in the United States. Despite state-by-state variations, our system for the governance of local schools is one in which arrangements for the finance of schools essentially determine, not only the amount of resources provided, but the distribution of school services among pupils of differing social, economic, and scholastic characteristics as well, and even major aspects of the educational technology employed in implementing curriculum and instructional methods.

The system of governance of schools in the United States, then, is one in which finance is the major mechanism of system control. Local school authorities in the United States have extremely wide powers regarding the total amount to be spent, the particular input mix to be used, the distribution of resources among specific schools, types of schools to be made available within a community, the assignment of pupils to particular schools and to tracks within schools, the curriculum taught, the teaching methods and the instructional materials used, and even the general attitudes in the schools toward pupils as clients or as genuine participants.

Although state governments exercise some control over these aspects of schools through legislation and administrative regulations, such mechanisms of control are used in great moderation. Instead, where states and the federal government wish to influence the specific characteristics of schools operated by local authorities, they rely on conditional grants-in-aid. The current range and scope of educational grants-in-aid boggles the mind. In addition to the over thirty categorical programs administered by the U.S. Office of Education there are numerous conditional grant programs within the states. Grant conditions extend from the characteristics of the residents of the school authority (e.g., Title I of the ESEA), to particular subjects (e.g., science and languages), to types of instructional materials and techniques (e.g., language laboratories), to types of schooling (e.g., vocational aid). Thus, it seems fair to refer to the U.S. system as one in which finance determines the quantity and characteristics of the real resources devoted to local schools and their organization into school programs. The leverage of such grants-in-aid in influencing the nature of school programs is often enhanced by requirements that grants be matched by local funds.

Such a system has many striking features. President Nixon and other

New Federalists in the present Administration in Washington are impressed by the unwieldiness and lack of coordination in a system with so many alternative grant programs. Many economists, lawyers, and citizens are dismayed by the extremes of tax effort and expenditures which such a system creates. What is to me the most striking aspect of this structure, however, is that no other nation places primary responsibility for the regulation of local schools in financial mechanisms of control. Throughout the world and, more to the point, in the developed nations of Western Europe, countries rely essentially on legislation and administrative regulations to ensure that an education which meets national standards—specified generally in input terms—is provided to all children without undue burdens on particular localities. Once a nation or a federated unit of a federation establishes mandatory standards for its local schools, adequate finance must be provided to the authority which is responsible for the operations of the school. If this were not done, the local authority could not be compelled to meet the necessary standards.

It can be said that in countries whose system of local governance operates in this manner finance follows the establishment of educational standards and the essential features of the school system are established when government authorities, through legislation and ministerial orders, set forth the standards for the operation of local schools. Then, consistent with these requirements, the higher level of government provides schools with resources adequate to meet the standards, and budgets which are sufficient to accomplish these standards are enacted. Thus, finance is relegated to a residual status with respect to control.

If one accepts this broad generalization regarding the essential difference in the role of finance in school governance as it operates in the United States and in other developed nations, some important implications emerge. Most countries do not believe that financial mechanisms are adequate or even appropriate for controlling the educational services provided to their children and youth. They do not wish to allow the characteristics of local schools to be determined by the relative wealth of local authorities or by the preferences of local school administrators for, or even their responses to, financial incentives expressed in terms of grant conditions. The question for the governance of schools in the United States is whether reform should concentrate on the removal of obvious fiscal disparities, leaving the governmental structure which controls other dimensions of schools relatively unchanged. Since the present system relies so heavily on finance as a mechanism of control, this reform would leave us with a political and administrative structure ill adapted to its tasks. A major change in school finance away from categorical grants and other fiscal means of control would seem to require a more general reform of the entire system, especially if the objective is to deal with the problems of alienation, lack of learning, disruption, and boredom that seem so common in our schools. If reform beyond mere financial equalization is to take place, one needs to have an idea of the characteristics of organizational and administrative alternatives.

Background to Alternative Methods for Governance

What, then, are the fundamental alternative methods for the governance and control of a local service, such as schools? Before we can establish these alternatives and examine them in theory and practice, a few preliminary notions need to be developed. One is the question of in what sense schools are a local function. They are a local function partly for reasons of costs—it is cheaper for students to live and board at home—but mostly because it is believed that both children and society benefit from children's being brought up within the family rather than in the impersonal setting of a boarding institution. Consequently the teachers, administrators, and pupils who participate in a school enterprise reside relatively close to it; the local government within whose jurisdiction the school is located has significant responsibilities for its administration and operation; and an important portion of the school's costs usually passes through the local government's budget.

Essential tasks of a school system

Another bit of necessary background is a consideration of the school as an organization. All organizations, public or private, must have arrangements for handling three functions: (1) resource acquisition (they must acquire resources or inputs); (2) service distribution (they must determine the characteristics which their products or services will have and to whom these will be provided); and (3) technical capacity (they must establish a technology commensurate with their service provision). Schooling, it is almost universally agreed, should be compulsory up to a certain level. For this reason, if for no other, the use of decentralized prices and profit incentives as the basic method of performing the three necessary functions is unacceptable. Alternative methods which ensure that an organization will service all its clientele involve a measure of government initiative and political determination to see to it that these functions are in fact performed. It is extremely important to keep in mind, however, that the three elements in a social organization are distinct. The methods of control employed by an administrative or political agency to regulate one aspect may affect another. For example, methods for providing resources to schools may also influence the distribution of their services and the technology used within schools.

The essential point to keep in mind, then, as we review approaches to school governance, is that it is necessary not only to manage to provide adequate resources to local schools but also to regulate the character and distribution of school services and the technologies used in schools in a manner consonant with the aims and values of society or of particular elements of the society.

General methods of controlling local government service provision

Before turning to specific alternatives of systems organization, administration, and finance in local schools we may find it useful to expose the general implications of centralization versus decentralization as contexts within which local governments deliver services.

Let us start from the pole of complete decentralization. When fully decentralized local authorities have responsibility for provision of services the primary difficulties encountered are fiscal disparities and geographic spillovers. Under these circumstances to redistribute resources and promote efficiency some fiscal centralization is called for. But, if resources are provided from the center, how does the system ensure that the local authority is employing these resources in conformance with the objectives of the center as regards service delivery and techniques? An answer to this question, the one implicit in U.S. practice, is to place responsibility in the hands of locally elected officials and rely on the political process. Local politics, however, are not especially responsive to the needs of minorities and other noninfluential citizens or to the preferences of nonresidents whose welfare is affected by policies of nearby local governments. Furthermore, spillovers for such functional areas as education, safety, transportation, and health are not of equivalent spatial scope. As a consequence, problems associated with either metropolitanization or proliferation of government authorities arise.

The standard response to these difficulties is to tie intergovernmental grants to categorical or conditional requirements and to monitor conformance. But, here, new problems arise: (1) complexity becomes overwhelming; (2) unequal grantsmanship emerges; (3) there is distortion of local preferences; (4) inadequate funding makes the availability of grants uncertain even when the locality clearly meets established criteria; (5) program evaluation generally is not systematically carried out; and (6) the overall pattern of conditional grants may be contradictory and inconsistent.

These well-known difficulties with decentralization explain why centralization is the approach to the regulation of local services which is most frequently encountered throughout governments of the world. Centralization controls local service provision through legislation, central ministerial orders, field administrators, inspection, and administrative courts. The obvious shortcomings of this approach are the absence of variations to reflect local differences in circumstances and preferences and rigidity in the application of administrative and operational regulations.

The conflict between local autonomy, subject to conditional intergovernment grants, and centralized administration as means of control of local services arises anew in almost every generation. What is known as the New Federalism of the Nixon Administration provides a contemporary illustration. There is, however, another approach which recently has been receiving renewed attention. This approach can be applied only to those local public services where the service can be provided in different amounts and characteristics to different individuals or groups of individuals. Yet, for reasons of equity or externalities, it is viewed as appropriate that all citizens (or all citizens with certain characteristics) receive minimum quantities thereof. In this case, instead of a public authority's actually producing such services at a single, community-wide, uniform level and quality and providing them free of charge to community residents, a number of private suppliers, perhaps alongside public enterprises, might produce the service at equal resource input cost, but in different forms and characteristics. The government would provide equivalent finance to the various private producers so that individuals would be able to choose a particular supplier on the basis of his product, but citizens themselves would not pay for the services directly.

This proposed solution to the control of certain local government services has its shortcomings and difficulties. Economies of scale might make it a more costly approach in some cases; unquestionably there need to be administrative regulations of some sort to insure technical capacity and reasonable outputs. Still, in some areas, including local schools, it offers promise of a resolution which meets many of the major objections to both the administrative and political solutions.

Characteristics of Alternative School Organizations

When one thinks of school organization the common contrast is between centralized and decentralized arrangements. What are the essential features of centralized and decentralized systems of school governance? Let us start with the one with which we are most familiar—decentralization. What are the fundamental characteristics of a decentralized school organization?

Decentralization

Decentralization might easily be defined in such a way as to eliminate entirely the public character of school operation, reducing public involvement solely to subsidizing pupils, parents, or private school enterprises. If local schools are to remain essentially public enterprises, however, then full or extensive decentralization requires that no central authority administers or operates such schools or establishes the amount of resources provided to them, the nature and degree of differentiated types of schools, the selection of students, or the educational techniques and materials used. This said, the question remains: Under decentralization, who does do these things?

One answer is that local governmental authorities make all these decisions. Thus, the center, whether a national or state government, refrains from constraining local authorities in their school activities except as regards general constitutional guarantees of equal treatment and civil rights. Under this concept, the responsibility to schools is delegated to a general- or special-purpose local authority through its elected council or board. It is expected not only to provide resources out of assigned local sources of revenue but also to set standards for delivery and techniques and to operate the schools by hiring teachers and administrators and assigning them to particular schools or positions and by creating and maintaining the physical plant.

Decentralization might be extended to the individual school plant through the establishment of some sort of school-by-school governing body which would appoint the headmaster and teachers and determine basic approach to education within the school. Financial support to the individual schools would still be provided by the local authority according to uniform criteria, and school personnel would be its employees.

The local authority would have to have some control over the numbers of schools of various types (e.g. academic, vocational) and over criteria for the assignment of pupils to each school to prevent some schools from employing invidious methods of selection. At the same time, however, to extend meaningful decentralization to the individual school, opportunities must be retained for pupils to choose schools and for schools to be differentiated.

The most familiar objections to decentralized school organization center on the fiscal inequalities among local school authorities. Remedies here focus on increased centralization of finance. But the rub is that centralization of finance is seen as necessarily bringing in its wake central control of such other aspects of schooling as service delivery and techniques. Is this perception correct? First, let us look at what overall centralization of school governance implies in principle. Then we will observe it in practice and contrast it to practices in decentralized school systems.

Centralization

A fully centralized system of control over schools implies that resources, their conversion into school programs, and the distribution of these programs among categories of students are regulated by a central source. This source may be the central government of a unitary state or, with certain qualifications, the state or provincial government of a constituent unit of a federation. A stylized description of full centralization starts with the powers of the legislature and the central agency of school administration, usually called the ministry of education. In principle, the former specifies the general terms under which the service is to be produced and the conditions of its distribution. The ministry of education has responsibility for transforming legislative provisions into specific orders and instructions and for their implementation. To discharge this responsibility the ministry places field administrators in positions of authority over local schools. At the same time the general political and administrative activities of local governments in centralized systems also are set forth in legislation and implemented by administrators—in this case by the interior ministry. Thus, local administration of both general government and of such functional activities as schools are heavily supervised and even performed by personnel who derive their authority and their objectives from a central source. This arrangement greatly reduces conflicts regarding priorities among various local services, although potential problems of coordination do arise between the education and interior ministries and their local representatives.

In this setting, the overall amount of resources provided for schools is determined as part of national budgetary and economic policy. The specification of educational service levels and techniques made by the legislature and the education ministry contain prescriptions regarding the quantities and types of real resources to be used. Since the resources required for operating schools have, in effect, been mandated through the setting of national standards, the center is obligated to provide all, or virtually all, of the necessary inputs to those local authorities to which it assigns operational responsibility. These amounts, however, must be consistent with the overall requirements of national economic policy. If the amounts required by mandated standards are excessive in terms of such policy, the ministry modifies them until they are consistent with budget allocations.

Allocation of resources to individual localities takes two forms under centralized arrangements. In the more centralized version, the national ministry hires or purchases the necessary resources and distributes them, according to the established standards, to its field administrators in local educational authorities, who then assign them to individual school establishments. In the less centralized version, the ministry assigns funds according to a formula to its local administrators, who then obtain the specified resources within regulated standards and amounts and assign them to individual schools. To ensure that local policies conform to central directives national field administrators of the education ministry, including a school inspectorate, examine and evaluate the performance of both teachers and local administrators.

Regardless of the details of resources allocation, a centralized control system must regulate the production of its most costly and specialized input—teachers—especially because standards of technique and delivery are invariably specified in terms of numbers and types of teachers. Resources for the training of teachers are included in national budgetary appropriations, and teacher-training institutions are financed and regulated in the same manner as are primary and secondary schools. Because the pattern of types of school and their curriculum is specified for the nation as a whole, it is possible to train teachers for particular schools or curricula in highly differentiated and specialized institutions.

One further aspect of centralized systems of administration needs mention. To adjudicate the conformance of ministerial instructions to national legislation and to resolve questions of inconsistent, contradictory, or arbitrary administrative practices, centralized systems use the administrative court. These courts, which usually consist of a series of lower and higher divisions, ensure that ministries and their field administrators do not exceed the powers granted them by legislation, and their rulings establish a basis for uniform administrative practices throughout the country.

Patterns of Control in Western Europe

Now, what about actual school systems in operation? Is centralization of one aspect necessarily associated with centralization of others? What combinations of centralization and decentralization are observed in practice and how do they appear to be working? The shortcomings of comparisons between nations are legion, and such comparisons cannot substitute for analytic, quantitative studies of the relation between structures, conduct, and performances of social system. These comparisons are, however, necessary starting points for such studies, and they can provide important and challenging insights by giving one perspective on his own system.

As for the provision of resources to local schools, none of the Western European countries which I've studied provides funds to local school authorities without either strict legislative or administrative controls or a combination of the two. The United States is probably the only country in the world in which local authorities are given taxing powers and grants-in-aid and allowed to administer the funds with little or no direct supervision from field administrators of higher levels of government and without detailed regulations regarding school organization and operation.

Under federal governments

There are several patterns of control over school resources, service delivery, and techniques observed in Western Europe which depart from the U.S. model. First let us look at two of the European federal states—Austria and the Federal Republic of Germany. These states might be thought to operate in a manner similar to that of the United States because of the formal similarity of basic government structure. This expectation, however, is not borne out.

Austria, nominally a federal state, is an extremely attenuated one in all areas, including schools. Not only is there a central government ministry of education, but the ministry directly administers, operates, and finances all of the nation's nonvocational secondary schools. Vocational secondary schools are operated by the federated states and primary schools by the lowest tier of authorities, municipalities. Even here, however, resources, service delivery, and technology are controlled by the center, which pays for primary and vocational teachers—who must be nationally certified—regulates curriculum and instructional methods and appoints supervisory school directors in the various Austrian states, who are field administrators of the central ministry.

The Federal Republic of Germany has not legally weakened its federalism, as has Austria. However, in Germany traditional federalism has always placed the states in an administrative position in relation to the executive role played by the central government. Thus, while the states have constitutional responsibility for education, a Permanent Conference of State Ministers of Education develops specific school regulations which, by and large, are enacted by individual state legislatures. Common regulations of this sort extend to types of schools, curriculum, grades, criteria for pupil selection, teacher/pupil ratios, and instructional methods. Uniformity reigns despite the absence of legal authority by the central government.

These uniform agreements across states do not extend to finance or to administrative structures. But, since school standards as well as standards for other local services are similar not only within but across states, the FRG, by employing interstate equalizing formula grants and the central government special-purpose grants, ensures that all states have revenues adequate to meet minimum functional responsibilities. Each state sees to it that its local authorities are provided with the inputs necessary to meet state regulations on the content and character of schools. This distribution is accomplished mainly through the employment of teachers and their assignment to localities by state governments and through state approval and subsidy of school construction. Noninstructional current outlays for schools, however, are met out of local government revenues, which consist of local taxes plus general purpose grants-in-aid from the state. The detailed school regulations of state legislatures and education ministries are enforced by a state field administration, under the leadership of a county or city school superintendent, and by local government executives who are supervised by field administrators of the state government.

Clearly, then, federal organization of a nation is not synonymous decentralization of school governance. Constituent units of a federation can be administered as unitary governments, allowing their local authorities only minimal initiatives and autonomy. In the FRG and Austria centralization of finance is a direct and necessary consequence of centralization of service delivery and techniques. These two federations, thus, offer no model of a mixture of centralization and decentralization as regards the various elements of the school system. Interestingly enough, as we shall see, one must turn to unitary states for illustrations of mixed arrangements.

Centralism in Europe

France. France, of course, is the archetype of centralization. Even here, however, local school finance is not fully centralized or uniform. All teachers are employed by the national ministry of education and assigned to their posts. Responsibility for other current expenditures by primary schools falls upon the *communes*. Noninstructional costs in secondary schools are met according to different arrangements which for the most part impose burdens on the local community. Administration is through field staff of the ministries of education and interior, with a regional superintendent appointed by the ministry of education having major responsibility. School regulations are spelled out in great detail in legislation and ministerial orders, and a national inspectorate evaluates teachers and administrators whose promotions depend on favorable ratings. Capital outlays are proposed and financed locally but must be approved by the education ministry in accordance with its master plan. Approved projects are subsidized according to a formula based on local needs and financial capacity. Obviously, there is little room here for diversity.

Sweden. Sweden operates a system almost as thoroughly centralized as that of France. Two elements in Sweden's school system are worthy of consideration as mechanisms of response to negative aspects of centralization. The first is the use of periodic national commissions for drafting basic social legislation. Sweden's educational system, as those of most unitary states, is guided by legislation which sets out the structure of local schools in considerable detail. In Sweden such legislation is developed through national commissions, on which all interested parties, including technical experts, are represented. The commission makes a recommendation only after all participants agree to its substance. This approach to educational legislation is a sharp contrast to the French approach, where the ministry or legislature generally acts on the basis of recommendations from ministerial staff or special consultants, in many cases in direct conflict with teachers' unions, parents' groups, and others.

The second innovative feature of Swedish administration is the interposition of the National Board of Education between the national ministry and the provinces and municipalities which operate schools. Presumably free of partisan political consideration, the National Board is able to develop effective relations with local communities and, thereby, adapt regulations to local cirucmstances.

With these two exceptions Swedish education is typically centralized. Teachers are hired by local authorities (another contrast to France), who are reimbursed by the central government for their salaries according to national norms. Details of types of schools, curriculum, and teacher/pupil ratios are set either in legislation or in regulations of the National Board of Education, and regional officials of the NBE supervise local officials in their applications of administrative and legislative regulations.

France and Sweden offer little in the way of patterns of mixed decentralization and centralization, but Sweden's approach may suggest ways to reach agreement about provisions for nationwide school regulations and their subsequent administration.

Norway. Norway's system provides a fascinating illustration of the irrelevance of finance when the provision of the school services is specified uniformly in great detail. School techniques in Norway are centralized to a greater degree than in either France or Sweden. An agency of the Norwegian education ministry develops text books, instructional materials, and course syllabuses used uniformly throughout the country. Legislation and ministerial orders specify teacher/pupil ratios and school facilities. Field administrators of the central government supervise local schools. Yet school finance is provided through a system of variable matching grants from the central government. For five specific categories of school expenditures—e.g., teachers, transportation, facilities—different rates of matching local contributions, ranging from 30 to 85 percent, are in effect. The rate of matching varies not only with the category of educational spending but in relation to the fiscal capacity of the community.

In light of previous remarks that finance must follow resources where standards are mandated, how does the Norwegian arrangement manage to work? It works, apparently, because the central government's field administrators insist that local communities meet their mandates, and the terms of matching make it financially feasible for all communities to do so. Thus, in Norway matching grants do not serve as a means of central influence over resource use, but rather they are a method for equitable subsidization of centrally mandated school programs among local authorities of varying incomes and educational needs. One interesting feature of a Norwegian grant-in-aid is that, in an effort to promote local efficiency, it bases the amount of matching funds to be granted, not on the actual outlay in local expenditures, but on an amount determined by applying national standards of unit cost to the number of units of the service provided by the local community.

Mixed systems

Norway, then, provides an illustration of a mixed system where finance is relatively decentralized while delivery and technology are highly centralized. Are there situations in which finance is centralized and services and technology decentralized? The answer is yes, and the countries involved are England and Wales and the Netherlands.

Holland. Dutch society and culture are split rather sharply along denominational lines between Catholics and Protestants. As a result the conception of democracy that has evolved in the Netherlands stresses the rights of diverse groups to equal public support for their own organizations and activities wherever possible rather than attempting to reach consensus for a single, uniform set of public services. In education this tendency is manifested by a system in which state, denominational, and other private schools have equal access to public funds. Municipalities administer and operate state primary and secondary schools. In addition, denominational and nondenominational private schools receive support from central and local authorities equivalent to that provided to similar state-operated schools. As in most unitary states, teachers' salaries, uniformly set by nationwide collective bargaining, are supported by the central government while the municipality pays for noninstructional school costs. Since virtually all local revenues come from general grants from the central government, school finance is almost entirely centralized.

Within these wide opportunities for independent establishment of schools, however, central mechanisms of control do operate. First, while any bona fide group may organize a primary school with a minimum of twenty-five pupils and receive free premises and an operating subsidy, at secondary level the central government will subsidize new schools only if they conform to the education ministry's plan for priorities and only to the extent of the ministry's allowances for new public investment spending. Second, while nonstate schools are not required to conform fully to the detailed regulations of the Dutch state schools as regards curriculum and instructional methods, they are subject to certain state controls. The denominational schools have their own administrative and supervisory hierarchies, but their teachers must hold state certificates. There is also state inspection of private schools as regards both their performance standards and their financial audits. More importantly, school-leaving examinations, which determine entrance into higher education, are prepared by the national education ministry, and private as well as state schools adapt their programs to promote success in these examinations. As a result, those who have the most knowledge of the Dutch system are struck by its uniformity rather than by its diversity.

England and Wales. Freedom of private individuals to organize schools which are subsidized by the state, then, does not lead to diversity in the Netherlands. England and Wales, part of a unitary state, have no national regulations or even ministerial orders regarding school organization, curriculum, or technology. Each local educational authority (there are 162 of these, and they are essentially coterminous with general government authorities) operates and administers its schools through an elected council, the education committee of this council, and a chief education officer chosen by the council. However, these administrators and executives do not have the authority to set basic school policies for each school as does the school and superintendent of an American school district. These matters are reserved to the individual school, whose headmaster and lay board of governors or managers has the duty to establish the educational perspective and character of the school. Finally, within the school itself, the classroom teacher in his subject matter presentation is not bound to follow the recommendations of either the headmaster or the school inspectorate. Although details of techniques are left to the individual school, questions of service delivery are determined at the level of the local authority by the education committee. One result of this arrangement is that there is an uneven pattern of secondary school organization throughout the ministry.

The finance of this system is moderately centralized. The central government, unlike governments in other unitary states, does not pay for teacher's salaries nor are there special purpose educational grants to local authorities, as there are in the United States. Instead the central government makes a single general grant which includes elements to reflect local needs and fiscal equalization. The remainder of local revenues is derived from local property taxes. This system of finance does not eliminate substantial variation in local revenues. To prevent inordinate variations in resources available for schools, local authorities have agreed upon a teacher quota system, and school construction is regulated by the central department of education.

England and Wales thus illustrate another viable mixture of centralized and decentralized control of local schools. The central government ensures that a rough minimum of resources is available to all school authorities through (1) a general grant, (2) regulation of local school building in accordance with needs, and (3) prevention of gross inequities among authorities in teaching staffs through support of the quota system and nationally equivalent salary scales for teachers. Within a total set by the general grant plus locally raised property tax revenues, locally elected and appointed school officials allocate resources among individual schools according to criteria which vary from locality to locality but which are applied uniformly within authorities. The degree of differentiation among schools and the assignment of pupils to particular schools is largely determined by each local school authority. On the other hand, curricula and techniques of instruction are the responsibility of the individual school and are set by the school's board of governors or managers, the headmaster, and the classroom teacher. Regional certification examinations at secondary level do influence curricula, and there is a national school inspectorate, whose powers are, however, strictly advisory. England and Wales, then, combine strong elements of central finance with local authorities' regulation of service delivery and school-by-school control over techniques.

Conclusions

What can be concluded from this impressionistic and incomplete overview of alternative school governance systems which is relevant to the debate over school organization and finance in the United States?

Here are a few tentative conclusions, some of which go beyond matters discussed:

1. All other countries employ methods that ensure regional equality of resources to a greater extent than does the United States. None fails to guarantee school services at levels close to the national average at equal fiscal sacrifice to citizens, whatever their geographical location. This equality is achieved regardless of whether the mode of national government is a unitary or federal system.

2. Virtually all countries have found ways to incorporate what were originally independent, denominational schools into the state system of finance. This incorporation entails substantial regulation of these schools by governmental authorities but permits them some measure of autonomy.

3. In many countries equalization of educational resources is accompanied, indeed is a consequence of, centralized control over educational techniques and regulation of the types of school and the placement of pupils and teachers within them.

4. Those countries in which higher levels of government regulate school techniques and service delivery do not operate compensatory educational programs. That is, although they do have regulations which specify the characteristics of differentiated secondary schools and the criteria for pupil selection for these schools and they are able to specify special programs for handicapped or mentally disturbed children, they have not attempted to define the conditions which warrant special educational treatment for the socially, culturally, or economically deprived student.

It seems to me that this failure can be attributed to the inability, or perhaps unwillingness, of national legislatures to specify what deprivation is and what educational measures are necessary to cope with it. The ramifications for social policy of such specification by a national legislature are enormous and potentially highly disruptive. Where service delivery is decentralized so that identification of those qualified for compensatory education does not also require detailed specification of the appropriate educational services to be provided, compensatory programs do not contain the same political dynamite.

5. Some school systems, for example in the Netherlands and England and Wales, have combined central controls over resource provision with decentralized determination of techniques and service delivery. However, they employ methods for ensuring responsible behavior and utilization of the funds by local schools. These methods include teacher certification, highly professionalized teachers and school administrators, regionally or nationally uniform school-leaving or subject-matter examinations, a school inspectorate, a central education ministry with broad regulatory powers, including control over school construction, and, in the Netherlands, a highly centralized system of state schools operating alongside less-regulated, publicly supported, private schools.

6. No country combines centralization of finance with the complete absence of central influence over standards of service delivery. Obviously, we in the United States must find our own way toward equitable finance and increased options in the style and character of local schools. The experiences of other nations cannot show us the right way, but they can help us to avoid mistakes as we make the inevitable changes.

It is, therefore, instructive, if not conclusive, to observe the anomalous situation implicit in present proposals to centralize school finance to the state level and to provide special educational revenue-sharing to the states, while leaving the nonfiscal powers and responsibilities of local school authorities unchanged. Under these conditions local schools in the United States would be controlled neither by centralized regulation of service delivery and techniques nor by mechanisms for community development and acceptance of a variety of modes of schooling. Instead, local school authorities would have virtual *carte blanche* in the use of higher government revenues as regards almost all dimensions of schooling.

I hope my remarks have shown that there are many ways to achieve equity in school finance and a substantial reflection of the public interest in schooling without having to tolerate the monopoly over schools enjoyed by local boards of education and their appointees.

PREVIOUS VOLUMES IN THIS SERIES

The Future of Economic Policy, Myron H. Ross, Editor, 1966
Michigan Business Papers, No. 44

Paul W. McCracken	*The Political Position of the Council of Economic Advisers*
Robert Eisner	*Fiscal and Monetary Policy for Economic Growth*
Theodore W. Schultz	*Public Approaches to Minimize Poverty*
Jesse W. Markham	*Antitrust Policy After a Decade of Vigor*
Kenneth E. Boulding	*The Price System and the Price of the Great Society*
Robert Triffin	*International Monetary Reform*

Key Factors in Economic Growth, Raymond E. Zelder, Editor, 1967
Michigan Business Papers, No. 48

Martin Bronfenbrenner	*Japanese Economic Development in the Meiji Era, 1867-1912*
Nicholas Spulber	*Is the U.S.S.R. Going Capitalist?*
Milos Samardzija	*Economic Growth and Workers' Management in Yugoslavia*
Lauchlin Currie	*The Crisis in Latin American Development*
Edmundo Flores	*The Alliance for Progress and the Mexican Revolution*
Alexander Eckstein	*The Economic Development of Communist China*

The Cost of Conflict, John A. Copps, Editor, 1968
Michigan Business Papers, No. 51

Kenneth E. Boulding	*The Threat System*
Thomas C. Schelling	*The Diplomacy of Violence*
Seymour Melman	*The Price of Peace*
Murray L. Weidenbaum	*Towards a Peacetime Economy*
Roger E. Bolton	*National Defense and Regional Development*
Emile Benoit	*Economic Adjustments to Peace in the Far East and to Ending the Arms Race*

America's Cities, Wayland D. Gardner, Editor, 1969
Michigan Business Papers, No. 54

Wilbur R. Thompson	*The Process of Metropolitan Development: American Experience*
Hugh O. Nourse	*Industrial Location and Land Use in Metropolitan Areas*
Richard F. Muth	*The Economics of Slum Housing*
Dick Netzer	*Urban Government Finance and Urban Development*
Werner Z. Hirsch	*The Urban Challenge to Governments*

Antitrust Policy and Economic Welfare, Werner Sichel, Editor, 1970
Michigan Business Papers, No. 56

Walter Adams	*The Case for a Comprehensive and Vigorous Antitrust Policy*
Jules Backman	*Holding the Reins on the Trust Busters*
Almarin Phillips	*Antitrust Policies: Could They Be Tools of the Establishment?*
Richard B. Heflebower	*The Conglomerate in American Industry: A Special Antitrust Wrinkle*
Jesse W. Markham	*Structure versus Conduct Criteria in Antitrust*
William G. Shepherd	*Changing Contrasts in British and American Antitrust Policies*

Economic Policies in the 1970s, Alfred K. Ho, Editor, 1971
Michigan Business Papers, No. 57

James M. Buchanan	*Economists, the Government, and the Economy*
Martin Bronfenbrenner	*Nixonomics and Stagflation Reconsidered*
David I. Fand	*Some Observations on Current Stabilization Policy*
Gardner Ackley	*International Inflation*
Harry G. Johnson	*Inflation: A "Monetarist" View*
Bela Balassa	*Prospects and Problems of British Entry into the Common Market*

The Economics of Environmental Policy, Frank C. Emerson, Editor, 1973
Michigan Business Papers, No. 58

Joseph L. Fisher	*An Introduction to Environmental Economics*
Lester B. Lave	*The Economic Costs of Air Pollution*
Robert H. Haveman	*The Political Economy of Federal Water Quality Policy*
William S. Vickery	*The Economics of Congestion Control in Urban Transportation*
Jerome Rothenberg	*The Evaluation of Alternative Public Policy Approaches to Environmental Control*

51 293

82-5-354N.C.